THE KATRINA BOOKSHELF

Kai Erikson, Series Editor

In 2005 Hurricane Katrina crashed into the Gulf Coast and precipitated the flooding of New Orleans. It was a towering catastrophe by any standard. Some 1,800 persons were killed outright. More than a million were forced to relocate, many for the remainder of their lives. A city of five hundred thousand was nearly emptied of life. The storm stripped away the surface of our social structure and showed us what lies beneath—a grim picture of race, class, and gender in these United States.

It is crucial to get this story straight so that we may learn from it and be ready for that stark inevitability, *the next time*. When seen through a social science lens, Katrina informs us of the real human costs of a disaster and helps prepare us for the events that we know are lurking just over the horizon. The Katrina Bookshelf is the result of a national effort to bring experts together in a collaborative program of research on the human costs of the disaster. The program was supported by the Ford, Gates, MacArthur, Rockefeller, and Russell Sage Foundations and sponsored by the Social Science Research Council. This is the most comprehensive social science coverage of a disaster to be found anywhere in the literature. It is also a deeply human story.

LEFT TO CHANCE

HURRICANE KATRINA AND THE STORY OF TWO NEW ORLEANS NEIGHBORHOODS

STEVE KROLL-SMITH, VERN BAXTER,
AND PAM JENKINS

University of Texas Press

AUSTIN

Requests for permission to reproduce material from this work should be sent to:
Permissions
University of Texas Press
P.O. Box 7819
Austin, TX 78713-7819
http://utpress.utexas.edu/index.php/rp-form

⊚ The paper used in this book meets the minimum requirements of
ANSI/NISO Z39.48-1992 (R1997) (Permanence of Paper).

LIBRARY OF CONGRESS CATALOGING-IN-PUBLICATION DATA

Kroll-Smith, Steve, 1947– author.
Left to chance : Hurricane Katrina and the story of two New Orleans
neighborhoods / Steve Kroll-Smith, Vern Baxter, and Pam Jenkins. — First edition.
pages   cm
Includes bibliographical references and index.
ISBN 978-1-4773-0369-6 (cloth)
ISBN 978-1-4773-0384-9 (pbk.)
ISBN 978-1-4773-0386-3 (non-lib. ebook)
ISBN 978-1-4773-0385-6 (ebook)
1. Hurricane Katrina, 2005.   2. Disaster victims—Louisiana—New Orleans.
3. Racism—United States.   4. United States—Race relations.   5. Social classes—
Louisiana—New Orleans.   6. Neighborhoods—Louisiana—New Orleans.   I. Baxter,
Vern K., author.   II. Jenkins, Pamela, author.   III. Title.
HV6362005.N4 K76 2015
976.3′35064—dc23   2014036203

doi: 10.7560/303696

Dedication

To all who struggled to remake their lives in the wake of this historic flood, we owe you our deepest gratitude; you've earned our deepest respect. And to Amanda, who left us far too soon, be assured darlin', your spirit continues.

CONTENTS

ACKNOWLEDGMENTS

In the seemingly endless path between beginning to research and write this book and finishing what we started, many people appear and in their own ways lend a hand.

Steve took inspiration from Susan, Emma, Brett, Leo, and Betty Lu. Thank you.

Among those who made significant contributions are Kai Erikson and Carol Stack. Two former graduate students and now junior faculty at the University of North Carolina, Greensboro, also provided important help along the way: Amy Ernstes and Tina Spach. We want to thank Kevin Brown, executive director of Trinity Christian Community Center; the Reverend Earl Williams; and Howard Rodgers, executive director of Orleans Parish Council on Aging. Lori Peek, Art Murphy, and Pete Kellett commented on various drafts and proposed book titles along the way. Our thanks to each of you.

And each of us found tenacity and wisdom in the many conversations we had with various people throughout this research. Among them are Cheryl Hayes, Bo Green, Jolinda Johnson, Diane Wooden, Denise Ancar, Pearly and Janet Harris, Jessie Green, Alayna Miller, and Michael Carey. And finally, we want to thank the Bill and Melinda Gates Foundation for providing the initial funding that got this project off the ground.

FOREWORD

Hurricane Katrina struck New Orleans at the beginning of the twenty-first century. Her winds and waters stirred up the history of this fabled city. Disasters generally have a way of making the past present, and this one was no exception. It did not take long to see that Katrina and the flooding of the city threw New Orleans' ugly race history into sharp relief.

During antebellum times being "sold down the river," namely, the Mississippi River, was a source of profound worry for blacks. New Orleans, the end point down the river, was imagined to be a city of sorrows. It was an abyss, a den of wickedness; it was thought to be the worst place a person could be sent. The horror of being sold down the river is a theme sounded in literature and oral tradition. In *Uncle Tom's Cabin*, the eponymous character meets his death at the run-down plantation of Simon Legree, down the river in rural Louisiana.

It is worth recalling that by 1840 New Orleans was the center of the slave trade in the United States. In his autobiography, *Twelve Years a Slave*, Solomon Northup recounts a slave auction in the Vieux Carré. In vivid prose he describes this dehumanizing moment—the slave pens, the wrenching apart of families, the horror of it all. Summoning words from somewhere within, Northup concludes his account with this telling afterthought: "It was a mournful scene indeed."[1]

"It was a mournful scene indeed" is a string of words that spans the wretched misery of the nineteenth-century slave auction and that catastrophic moment more than 160 years later when tens of thousands of black families lost everything, some even life itself. White people living in New Orleans also suffered, of course. But they could weather their misery in the absence of that ornery consciousness described by W.E.B. Du Bois as the double: "one ever feels his two-ness, an American, a Negro; two souls . . . two unreconciled strivings; two warring ideals."[2]

As Katrina made its way to New Orleans, Mayor Ray Nagin issued the first mandatory order to evacuate in the history of the city. It is worth setting the demographic and temporal context for the mayor's order. When Katrina slammed into the eastern edge of the Paris of the South, more than half of the population of New Orleans was black. Moreover, New Orleans ranked eighth among American cities with the poorest populations. Twenty-eight percent lived below the poverty line. Fourteen percent of city residents lived in households with incomes below 50 percent of the poverty line. Upward of 40 percent of the population was functionally illiterate. By 2005, in short, the legacy of slavery and racism combined with the deindustrialization of the American economy had left an indelible mark on the material circumstances of most blacks living in New Orleans.[3]

Now, consider the date that the mayor issued his evacuation order: August 28, the end of the month. For folks living below, at, or just above the poverty line, money was in short supply in the last few days of August. Who could afford to evacuate became a question rooted in the history of the city. The best many people could do was seek refuge on their roofs. Many stayed there for days. Some didn't make it, perishing from the punishing heat and lack of food and water. In many ways Hurricane Katrina was a perfect storm throwing into stark relief the consequences of long years of racial oppression, a mutating economy, and, as this book documents, a failed federal relief effort.

Left to Chance steps boldly into this fray. The authors look closely and over a long period at the experiences of residents in two historic New Orleans neighborhoods, both African American: Hollygrove and Pontchartrain Park. The first is a working-class enclave reclaimed from swamp sometime in the 1920s. Subject to the whims of city planners, major thoroughfares slice through this neighborhood, giving it a haphazard look and feel, as if what is there is simply what is left after others make decisions about how best to travel by car.

The second neighborhood is what we would call middle class. Pontchartrain Park is a testament to Homer Adolph Plessy, a former New Orleanian whose arrest for violating a race segregation law in Louisiana led to the famed Supreme Court decision *Plessy v. Ferguson*. Developed in the 1950s to accommodate a small but rising middle-income class of blacks, Pontchartrain Park was designed to comply with the "separate but equal" clause of the 1896 decision. In short, both neighborhoods are shaped by the shifting fortunes of race tied to class in this iconic American city.

The authors open a wide space for the voices of those who lived with and through the flooding of the city. Behind their stories is the inescapable shadow of race and its partner, class, there for any reader to see. From the first moments when evacuating or staying put is a decision that must be made, to the pitiful state and federal relief efforts, to years later when life once again begins to take on the appearance of the normal, we are brought face to face with the chaotic world of disaster. It is a world—as the voices in this book make unmistakably clear—in which chance is in charge.

Following the lives of men and women in these two neighborhoods for several years after that fateful day in August 2005, Kroll-Smith, Baxter, and Jenkins weave a compelling account of people working against the odds to make sense of and manage the protracted and bewildering mess that was, and in many ways still is, Hurricane Katrina.

Elijah Anderson, William K. Lanman, Jr.
Professor of Sociology at Yale University

LEFT TO CHANCE

PROLOGUE

Someone who has experienced a disaster that takes lives, destroys houses, and leaves survivors without a discernible path to recovery is likely to find little surprising in a story that connects calamity to the unforeseen. But such a story is at odds with a good deal of that social science literature on disasters proffering models, management strategies, and explanations in a bid to tame these feral events. Such constructs and classifications are meant to sweep the shards of a deranged world into a pile, "converting," to borrow the good words of Charles Perrow, "micro-confusion into macro-order."[1] Our scholarly effort to domesticate disaster has a long, some might say divine history. Recall for a moment that well-known Judeo-Christian Flood.

Was God the first disaster planner? He certainly knew what was coming. It was, after all, his doing. But by his own account he could not command the Flood without also instructing at least one person on what and how to prepare to survive it. It is arguably in the first book of the Bible that disaster and planning begin what has become an enduring relationship. Anticipating—albeit with imagination—a twenty-first-century disaster-preparedness official, God instructs Noah on preparing for a flood:

> Make for yourself an ark of gopher wood; you shall make the ark with rooms, and shall cover it inside and out with pitch. And this is how you shall make it: the length of the ark three hundred cubits, its breadth fifty cubits, and its height thirty cubits. You shall make a window for the ark, and finish it to a cubit from the top; and set the door of the ark in the side of it; you shall make it with lower, second, and third decks. . . . [A]nd you shall enter the ark—you and your sons and your wife, and your sons' wives with you. . . . [T]ake for yourself some of all food which is edible . . . and gather it to yourself; and it shall be for food for you and for them.[2]

Could God not create a disaster without also creating a disaster plan? That question is best left to others whose knowledge and faith exceeds ours, though the Federal Emergency Management Agency (FEMA) might want to pay attention to the detail in God's instructions. What we do know is that the alliance between disaster and planning foreshadowed in ancient scripture has survived the ages, becoming over time a durable pact. The one term now follows the other—with no hint of irony—in the juxtaposition of calamity and mayhem on the one hand with reason and order on the other. In fact, the word "disaster" is used as much or more as an adjective modifying "planning" or "management" as it is used as a noun standing on its own. The lexicon of management and planning would tame it, assigning some teleological path from, by one account, "pre-emergency" to "emergency" to "restoring normality" and finally, to "recovery."[3] Much of what the social science of disaster has taught us derives from the spinning out of possibilities implicit in these kinds of terms.

Researching and writing with an eye to discovering stages and systemic patterns across a comparable range of extreme events makes good sociological and applied sense. Our quarrel with this way of seeing disaster is that it is also a way of not seeing disaster. Ken Hewitt had something like this in mind when he invoked the playwright Bertolt Brecht to indict the normal social science approach to calamity for failing "to recognize how the roots and occurrence of contemporary disasters depend upon the way 'normal everyday life turns out to have become abnormal, in a way that affects us all.'"[4]

Our stages, systemic patterns, and abstractions are akin to maps, simplifications of those terrains we seek to navigate. To get us from here to there, a map must eschew the incidental and the particular. A map that included every detail would likely get us lost or at least confused.[5] But what if the devil, as it were, is in those details? We might ask how many idiosyncratic and original human experiences of life in calamity are hidden from sight under blanket terms like the "emergency period" or "restoring normality"? The idea of restoring normality, for example, discourages us from a studied look at the chance-ridden life in disaster, directing our attention instead to the triumph of reason in the management of chaos.

In writing this book we try not to look away from madness toward the saneness of the first-this-then-that. We took direction from William James, who celebrated the out of the ordinary. In his well-chosen words, "There is a zone of insecurity in human affairs in which all the dramatic interest lies."[6] Faced with insane nature joined to a massive failure of federal, city, and state resolve, what's left is a raw, elemental uncertainty and an elusive belief that it might be overcome. But what if the knowledge we do not know and cannot readily access is essential to us?

We will take a deliberate look at contingency and chance as they worried the lives of residents in two historic New Orleans neighborhoods. We will dwell at some length in that "zone of insecurity," the inversions, the gaps, and anomalies created by a historic flood and the troubled relief efforts that followed. We continue and elaborate on the idea of chance and its relation to social and cultural studies in the epilogue.

INTRODUCTION
WATER, CONVERSATIONS, AND RACE

Any Thing is said to be contingent,
or to come to pass by Chance
or Accident . . . when its Connection
with its Causes or Antecedents,
according to the establish'd Course
of Things, is not discerned.

JONATHAN EDWARDS, 1754

In 1718 the governor of French Louisiana, Jean-Baptiste Le Moyne de Bienville, made what we might call today an executive decision.[1] Against the advice of the regent's royal engineers and the regent himself, Bienville sited a new outpost on a plat of high ground that would later be called the Vieux Carré. In a letter to Regent, Philippe, the Duc d'Orléans, Bienville made a case for the site as a valuable find on this riverine corridor, with the Mississippi River on one side and swamp draining into a massive lake on the other. Tellingly—and with a practiced talent for flattery—he called this dry land surrounded on all sides by water "l'isle de la Nouvelle Orléans," the island of New Orleans.[2]

A year later, in 1719, Sieur de Bienville wrote again reporting that the Mississippi River regularly overflowed her banks, leaving his newest discovery under a half foot of water. It was, after all, in his words, an island. Levees and drainage canals were needed, he opined.[3] The royal engineers could not be blamed for smiling just a little on receipt of this news. They knew what many later inhabitants of the region would over time forget and others would simply take in stride: as cypress swamps were backfilled and bayous drained, New Orleans would become what one urban historian has called "the accidental city."[4]

In the best of times living in New Orleans is a dicey proposition, and while there are many forces at play contributing to a palpable sense of the precarious, surely one thing ruinous to a settled way of life is an unstable environment. It is estimated that roughly half of present-day New Orleans sits above sea level and half below. Approximately ten square miles of the city rests level with the sea.[5] It is not uncommon to walk near the Mississippi River in the Algiers Point neighborhood and glance up beyond the rooflines of the shotgun houses to see a ship whose bow soars ten to twenty feet above you, gliding as if on air rather than water.

To make matters even soggier, sixty-four inches or more of rain falls on New Orleans annually. Rainfall above one-half inch per hour will typically exceed the capacity of the city's 148 drainage pumps, ensuring that streets, cars, and the occasional house will flood.[6] New Orleans rests on land a few feet below sea level that itself sits on a soggy chemical composition of one oxygen and two hydrogen atoms. Fickle and capricious, such a city slips easily from human control. It is, as some say, a "city in a bowl."

This vertical cross-section of the topography of the city shows how dependent New Orleans is on its levee system. It has a maximum levee height of twenty-three feet on the Mississippi River bank and ten feet on the bank of Lake Pontchartrain. Remove or damage either of the two levees and the bowl begins to fill. When water gets into the bowl, getting it out is no easy task.

Between 1816 and 2005, New Orleans experienced serious flooding on twenty-seven separate occasions.[7] In 1849 a breach on the east bank of the Mississippi several miles above New Orleans left the city awash in brown, fusty water for forty-eight days. Between 1849 and 1874, the city flooded four more times. Eight years later, in 1882, New Orleans was under floodwater for more than three months.[8]

Hurricane Betsy swept through the New Orleans area in September 1965, flooding 164,000 homes, 6,600 of them in New Orleans. One survivor of this billion-dollar storm recalls, "God, it was like one giant swimming pool as far as the eye could see. A woman who lives down the block floated past me, with her two children beside her."[9] In 1995, ten years before Katrina, twenty inches of rain fell in a single day, flooding approximately 20,000 homes and causing seven deaths and more than $1 billion in damage across three parishes, including Orleans.[10] But it would take a weak category 3 hurricane that glanced off the city's eastern flank to create the most devastating flood in New Orleans' almost three-hundred-year history.

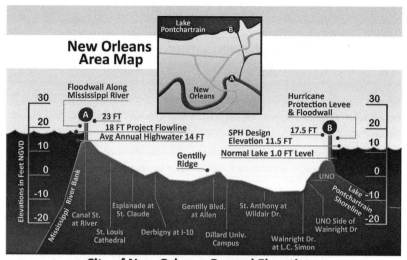

City of New Orleans Ground Elevations
From Canal St. at the Mississippi River to the Lakefront at U.N.O.

I.1. Vertical cross-section of New Orleans elevations. This image starkly depicts the now-commonplace idea that New Orleans lies at the bottom of a bowl between the Mississippi River on one rim (left, maximum levee height 23 feet) and Lake Pontchartrain on the other (right, maximum levee height 17.5 feet). As in an upright bowl, once water gets into the city it is difficult to remove. *Source*: Wikipedia, *Levee Failures in Greater New Orleans*, http://en.wikipedia .org/wiki/2005_levee_failures_in_Greater_New_Orleans.

Left to Chance is a close-up look at residents of two historic African American neighborhoods who put words and sentences together to tell about their many and varied experiences with "Miss Katrina" and all that followed. The moniker "Miss Katrina" was given to us by Jo Johnston of Pontchartrain Park. Without hesitation or even a raised eyebrow to signal a hint of self-awareness, Jo spoke of this storm and all that followed it as if it were someone she knew to be an unsavory person, a caller unbidden and bent on raising hell. We make use of Jo's expression at various places from chapter to chapter when we want to give this totalizing disaster a more personal, human form.[11]

Hollygrove is a working-class neighborhood situated on the western edge of the city. Pontchartrain Park is a middle-class enclave on the city's eastern edge, close to the lake from which it takes its name. Each settlement sits on what is sometimes called "liquid" or "made land," created when swamp was drained and backfilled with soil. Hurricane Katrina, in alliance with a woefully inadequate levee system, left each neighborhood under four to nine feet of water for roughly two weeks.

But nature, failed levees, and wild water were not yet finished with the city. On September 23, less than a month after Hurricane Katrina, winds from Hurricane Rita pushed yet more water into an already soaked city. A spokesman for the Army Corps of Engineers described it this way: "The areas being flooded at this time are, essentially, being reflooded. Rita simply overwhelmed the makeshift levees constructed after Katrina."[12] Flood levels, however, were well below those of Katrina.

In a short time, Rita was eclipsed in the public imagination by her far more potent sister. The people we spoke with in both neighborhoods rarely mentioned Rita. For them, and most everyone in the city, *the* disaster was Katrina. We follow suit and allow "Hurricane Katrina" to signify both storms.

The catastrophic flooding of New Orleans in late summer 2005 disordered lives and landscapes. But these waters did more than wreak havoc with the physical world; they seeped into a person's interior, putting at risk that innermost part of us. Some were left wondering what they meant when they said "I." As in, "What am *I* to do?" "Where am *I* going?" "How long will *I* be gone?" "How do *I* fix my everything?" For those tasked with remaking their lives, the winds, the waters they troubled, and the often Kafkaesque efforts at relief that followed conspired to create a seemingly interminable moment when lives skidded sideways, ruled more by happenstance than the predictable first-this-then-that of the reasonable.

We wrote this book to present and comment on the narrative accounts of people in two New Orleans neighborhoods who lived through these historic storms and the muddled relief efforts that followed. We did not interview with a well-defined schedule of questions that assumed what is worth knowing.[13] Rather, we made every effort to encourage each person we spoke with to talk about what life was like in the slip-sliding world of disaster.

People described passing from the familiar and routine into another, ominous world, one populated with mysteries, accidental encounters, adaptations, defeats, victories, and more. Their accounts of living on the edge, on the stretch, clinched and tense, fairly erupted off the hundreds of transcribed pages. They grappled with a world that Eric Hobsbawm puts into words while recalling some of the lasting echoes of World War I: "The past was beyond reach, the future postponed and the present bitter."[14]

We don't have a theory about their stories. Nor will we offer a bevy of concepts to tidy up the existential disorder narrated in the dozens of first-person accounts we collected over the past many years. The disorder that is disaster is far more accessible when it is attached not to generalized abstractions but to particular named people and the words they find to chronicle their trials, tribulations, and occasional victories on the makeshift road away from chaos.

Our goal in this book is to create a little disorder of our own. As we stand outside and look at the seemingly endless stream of pickles and jams that beset the residents of two neighborhoods, Hurricane Katrina invites us to write the surprising and unforeseen into the literature on disaster. We place front and center the "blooming, buzzing confusion" of disaster as it is remembered by the residents of Hollygrove and Pontchartrain Park.[15] If this book has a lineage, it is closer to the family of the heart than of the head. It is written for anyone who can understand and share the feelings of another. If this book were a letter addressing the audience we had in mind while writing it, the salutation might well read, "To Whom It May Concern."[16]

Read one way, *Left to Chance* is a litany of memories, a collection of recollections gathered over a five-year period beginning in the winter of 2005. It is in this way an oral history, one in which the authorship is shared among those who told us about disaster and the three of us who have edited and commented on their accounts. In this collaborative telling we bring to public attention the disordering forces of unleashed water on the one hand and the often greater chaos created by a disaster-assistance culture favoring a privatized response model on the other.

If understanding remains a worthwhile pursuit among those of us who study disaster, one place it is surely found is in the words people use to bring to life the thousands of tiny moments that make up their experiences of escaping, returning, rebuilding, and starting over. If we are seeking answers to the most human of questions—our "why? how? what? wither?"—they are likely "to be found," as Geertz knew well, "in the fine detail of lived life."[17] We seek, in sum, to write about real people in real places making whatever sense they can of a real nasty disaster.

SO MANY CONVERSATIONS,
SOME NOTES ON "BEING THERE"

Each of us, Steve, Vern, and Pam, has far more than an academic relationship with this disaster. Pam and her husband and Vern and his family lived through, and in some ways continue to live with, Hurricane Katrina. Steve's daughter, Amanda, and her husband also lived in New Orleans at the time of the flood. All three families evacuated, spent some time in exile, and struggled with disaster assistance, insurance companies, building contractors, and more. In short, each of us had a personal relationship with this historic disaster.

We had several conversations, deliberating on how we might write about it. Inevitably, these talks would come back to how Pam and Vern navigated the craziness of disaster, skidding from here to there in the concerted effort to make sense of it all. Steve would fill in with stories of his daughter and son-in-law. We spent hours talking to each other about the personal details of evacuating, finding long-term housing when return to New Orleans was not possible, accessing disaster assistance, rebuilding, and so on. We were a small community of survivors passing information back and forth, trading experiences, helping one another.

From day one, we each brought an eyewitness passion to this research. Fieldworkers who venture to other places with the goal of reporting on their travels face the task of convincing others that they, in Geertz's effortless phrase, "have been there." Their aim is to write in such a manner that a reader can say, "Had I been there I would 'have seen what they saw,' heard what they heard, 'felt what they felt, concluded what they concluded.'"[18] Vern and Pam are themselves survivors of the mayhem wrought by this hurricane. Steve was but a step away. Together, we brought a first-person intensity to this work. We were "there." Our here is the "there" we seek to bring to your attention.

It took us little time to recognize that what we wanted to do more than anything was listen carefully to the accounts of people who lived with and through the mayhem. More like confederates than interviewers, we paid close attention as each person spoke, piecing together their personal accounts, their tellings. Each of us, for our own personal reasons, wanted to hear the stories of others who slogged through this flood and all that followed. We also knew in our discipline of sociology that for those who live in disaster, theirs are often unwritten lives.[19]

Over the course of five years we conducted a series of sixty-eight extended conversational interviews with residents of both neighborhoods, taking anywhere between one and two hours apiece. We asked each person who spoke with us if we could record and transcribe the conversation. We read and reread these transcripts, often transfixed by the strength of the words. In addition to these recorded conversations, we paid social visits to residents of the two neighborhoods, picking up bits and pieces of the continuing stories of life in disaster.

All the people we interviewed had to rebuild. When we first visited them, some lived in FEMA trailers perched on their properties or on streets fronting them. We watched as they moved from their 250-square-foot Cavaliers to the first one or two rebuilt rooms in their houses. Some, unable to secure FEMA trailers, simply moved into their broken houses as they worked on them. Others lived hours from the city, driving back and forth to work on their properties. As the years went by, many people we interviewed took us on "new" house tours, pointing to their new furniture, artwork, colors for their walls, bathrooms, and dishes.

Beyond the five-year interview period we continued to visit the neighborhoods and speak with people informally for two years. Over time we developed personal relationships with a few of the people from Hollygrove and Pontchartrain Park. Driving through both neighborhoods, for example, we would stop occasionally and engage in that old New Orleans' custom of "porch sitting" with Jesse Gray, or we might stop in uninvited just to say "Hello" to Clara Carrington or Cheryl Haden, a greeting that might segue into a coffee and a chat.

Vern, a man who knows his way around the kitchen, cooked up some jambalaya now and then and dropped it by folks in Hollygrove who were going through particularly hard times. As we write these words, we have known many of these people for seven years, some less. During that time, we've had occasion to follow them as they settled their accounts with Miss Katrina. For a few, life ran out before they could find their way to the other side of this disaster. Bo from Hollygrove died more than a year after the flood. Clara from Pontchartrain Park died almost eight years after that fateful day in late August 2005. But for most of the people we interviewed over the past many years, Miss Katrina lives on, reminding them and us that in some tangible ways this flood never truly ends.

We made the decision to talk with people in two neighborhoods to throw into relief some of the fundamental economic and social differences found in this iconic Deep South city. Hollygrove is composed of low-, lower-middle-, and some middle-class households. This African American neighborhood has, for the most part, been invisible in the larger public story of Hurricane Katrina. More than seven years after the flood, a few houses were raised three or more feet off the ground; some were rebuilt to the same height that could not withstand the surge of the flood in the first place, as if tempting fate to try once again to destroy them. There were a few FEMA trailers left that residents were able to purchase, notorious reminders of an endless disaster. Other houses sit as if it were still August 29, 2005; they have not been gutted or fixed. They sit abandoned by their owners and the city.

Pontchartrain Park was created for middle-class African Americans, the first of its kind in the United States. The houses are primarily brick ranch style set on concrete slabs, built when the suburb was created in the 1950s. The floodwaters did not move houses off their foundations; it simply found its way inside and, more often than not, rose to the ceilings, remaining in place for the better part of two weeks. What strikes us as we drive through the neighborhood so many years after the water is the number of abandoned houses and the stillness that comes when people leave and never come back.

A considerable amount of time was spent gaining access to these diverse and complex neighborhoods. We gained entrée to Hollygrove through four portals: contacts made through Trinity Christian Community Center, an anchor at the edge of Hollygrove; the Hollygrove Food and Farm Network; the Hollygrove-Dixon Neighborhood Association; and residents of a four-block stretch of Forshey and Belfast Streets in Hollygrove. In some ways the Hollygrove neighborhood is more diverse than Pontchartrain Park. Income and age are distributed unevenly in this working-class "faubourg," a local term meaning "neighborhood." To address this greater diversity we recorded forty-seven conversations with a variety of people who call Hollygrove home. These more formal discussions were complemented by more than two dozen informal chats with Hollygrove residents.

We entered Pontchartrain Park through four avenues as well: the Pontilly Neighborhood Association; faculty contacts at Southern University of New Orleans, a historically black public university in the northern tier of the neighborhood, and at the University of New Orleans; the executive director of the Council on Aging, who has strong ties to both Pontchartrain Park and Hollygrove; and the Pontchartrain Park Senior Center. With greater demographic uniformity among residents of "the Park," we began to notice within fifteen or so conversations a pattern of reiterated themes. We recorded twenty-one conversations and took notes from more than a dozen informal discussions with residents of this neighborhood.

We began our inquiry by talking with thirteen residents, seven in Hollygrove and six in Pontchartrain Park. Each person talked about the history of his or her neighborhood. They spoke about what life was like in Hollygrove or the Park before the storm. But it was the flood, the water, the fear, the confusion, the anger, and more that people most wanted to talk about. And talk they did, not in the sense of a passive reply to a survey question, but as people animated by the need to give an accounting of their personal and up-close experiences with all that became for them Hurricane Katrina. The first several conversations were transcribed and coded. We then developed a list of themes that followed, roughly, their linear experiences of the disaster from pre-Katrina to their efforts to rebuild.

We collected historical and demographic data on each neighborhood, including maps, pre-Katrina census figures, and narrative descriptions. On many occasions we drove through the neighborhoods to get a visual sense of who returned, who was rebuilding, who was in a FEMA trailer, who was still living away from their homes, and so on. We often stopped and walked the streets to get a close-up look at the morphing social and physical contours of each locality. Finally, we attended neighborhood meetings, visited community centers, and took photographs. These many threads of contextual data gave us a sense of the whole cloth of Pontchartrain Park and of Hollygrove.

Throughout the book you will encounter many names. We wanted to personalize the stories we were told rather than use a more distant, frosty, impersonal approach. At the same time, for a variety of reasons, we chose not to use people's real names. We use pseudonyms throughout the text. Still, we've little doubt that the people in Hollygrove and Pontchartrain Park will recognize themselves and perhaps their neighbors in the pages to follow.

A NOTE ON RACE IN THE FIELD

All of the people who spoke with us in the course of this study are, in the tortured lexicon of race in the United States, African American. Each author is white. The caustic construct of race in most American cities is never far from the surface of human affairs; this is particularly true of cities in the Deep South. In chapter 1 we address the question of how race figured into the ways people in the two neighborhoods made sense of this disaster. But before we bring this introduction to a close, it is worth asking how the long-standing American preoccupation with the color of one's skin intersected with our fieldwork.[20]

We began the work in Hollygrove. In several thick descriptions of the history of the neighborhood, people spoke freely and without prompting about the confluence of black and white. To follow is one passage from an extended conversation with Joseph Shearman. His candid recollections of the politics of color while growing up in his neighborhood echo the direct, apparently unfiltered way race is talked about in this working-class faubourg. Recalling a moment growing up, Mr. Shearman puts words to a complex world of color in this part of New Orleans:

> It was around Thanksgiving and we were out there playing football, blacks against whites, and a couple of times people stopped on the overpass and

yelled at me, "I'm gonna tell your mama. You're playing with them. . . ." Yes, in the late '50s people from all over the city would come back here [to Hollygrove] and play football on Monday nights. . . . We'd have big games, and you know, there were high school players.

Mr. Shearman grew up in a color-coded world. Colors—black, white, and shades in between—are a conscious part of Joseph's life story. His story is common.

Michael Carrington, a successful accountant, lives in Pontchartrain Park. He talks about race in a more critical and less personal manner than Mr. Shearman does. And yet his words convey a man comfortable with the topic and his audience:

I guess when I look at it, we still live in a very race-conscious society. . . . [The O. J.] Simpson case, if you don't understand it, it was all about race. The verdict and people's reaction to it was really about race. It really wasn't about whether he did it or not. I'm one of those people that think if he didn't do it, he certainly knew something or was involved in some way. This was a verdict about race relations in this country, in my humble opinion. For blacks it was about whether it would even the score. It wouldn't. It couldn't. . . . Personally, I think . . . we haven't gotten that far in our race relations in the country.

A man who thinks about race, Michael's account was clipped and declarative, almost as if he were speaking to high school civic students. If our skin color mattered to him, it was perhaps to stress a point or two that he wanted us, as students of disaster, to understand.

These two brief narratives are offered to make the simple point that the people we interviewed knew well that they are African American and we are white. This difference—so plain and obvious—did not prevent them from inviting us time and again onto their porches and into their trailers and houses to talk about the trials, tribulations, and triumphs of life challenged by disaster.

A PREVIEW

To follow are seven chapters. The first six are divided into three parts. Part I, "Navigating Contingency in Two Historic Neighborhoods," includes chapters 1 and 2. Chapter 1, "'Katrina Takes Aim,'" sets out our particular way of looking at this disaster, placing front and center the marked confusion of living tethered to calamity. In "Geographies of Class and Color," chapter 2, we take the reader on a tour of Hollygrove and Pontchartrain Park, paying close attention to the topographical, historical, and social characteristics of these two historic neighborhoods.

Part II, "From Evacuees to Exiles," is comprised of two chapters. Chapter 3, "Life on the Road," is a close-up discussion of life lived in evacuation. "From the Road to Exile," chapter 4, follows the trials people faced in fashioning a place from which to survive the seemingly interminable period before returning to the city.

"Traversing and Rebuilding," Part III, begins with chapter 5, "It's Available, but Is It Accessible? Traversing the World of Disaster Assistance." Here we enter an arguably surreal space where little appears as it truly is. Chapter 6, "Rebuilding in a Broken City," follows the circuitous and maze-like paths people took to rebuild their damaged homes in a city whose local government was all but in a coma.

Our final chapter, "'The Katrina Effect': Is There a Coda?" relies on the voices of several people who were asked to appraise their relative well-being years after the flood. Their accounts of life postflood help us to make a case for revising or, at least, reappraising the idea of "disaster recovery." It is, quite frankly, a term with insufficient reach to grasp the meanings of the many stories we were told in the making of this book.

In the epilogue, "Making a Space for Chance," we address our colleagues in sociology and kindred fields who study and write about disaster. You are welcome to attend to these few pages. But be advised, they will not add anything to the substance of our discussion in the body of the book. Their purpose is to draw attention to the ideas underlying our look at the place of chance in accounting for the human response to disaster and, we hope, to open up a small space for this line of inquiry into the social, cultural, and psychological study of calamity.

I

NAVIGATING CONTINGENCY IN
TWO HISTORIC NEIGHBORHOODS

"KATRINA TAKES AIM"

Midway upon the journey of . . . life
I woke to find myself in a dark wood,
where the right road was wholly lost and gone

DANTE ALIGHIERI, "INFERNO: CANTO I"

On the morning of August 29, 2005, Katrina made landfall on the Gulf Coast as a category 3 hurricane; it packed sustained winds of roughly 125 miles per hour. As the eye of the storm made its way north, it veered to the east of New Orleans. Once again it appeared as though this fragile city, reclaimed from swamp and surrounded on three sides by water, was spared a direct hit. Residents, more than two-thirds of whom had evacuated the city ahead of the storm, breathed a sigh of relief. By early evening, however, water was rising in the bowl that is New Orleans, filling streets and lapping at the foundations of building and houses.[1]

The tidal surges from Katrina's winds were more than the city's ill-prepared levees could repel. By late in the day more than 80 percent of New Orleans was under water. It would be two weeks before the water retreated, leaving a wake of unimaginable destruction. The experts claimed time and again that the levees were built to withstand a category 3 storm. Lieutenant General Carl Strock, chief of engineers for the Army Corps, reported shortly after the dozens of levee breaches in New Orleans that the Corps "fully recognized . . . that we had Category Three level of protection" in New Orleans. He continued, "We were just caught by a storm whose intensity exceeded the protection that we had in place."[2] Weeks later Hurricane Rita would affirm, once again, the obvious: that water and New Orleans are well nigh synonymous. Both storms will be remembered far more as water than wind events.[3]

The flood destroyed, but it also created a surfeit of new and disorient-

1.1. A water-stained copy of the August 28, 2005, *Times-Picayune* in a vending machine outside the Plantation Coffee House, New Orleans. Photo by Steve Kroll-Smith, September 17, 2005.

ing postflood realities. Each of us knows what Pascal knew: ordinary life at times has "its reasons of which reason knows nothing."[4] But if the unforeseen and contingent haunt the margins of ordinary life, they move abruptly to the center in the deranged world of disaster.

Go back for a moment in time to Natchez, Mississippi. The year is 1927. The Mississippi River has topped its banks and flooded the delta lowlands. Richard Wright, a native of Natchez, imagines one family's return to a water-ravaged home:

> At last the flood waters had receded. A black father, a black mother, and a black child tramped through muddy fields, leading a tired cow by a thin bit of rope. They stopped on a hilltop. . . . As far as they could see the ground was covered with flood silt. The little girl lifted a skinny finger and pointed to a mud-caked cabin. "Look, Pa! Ain tha our home?" Without moving a muscle, scarcely moving his lips, he said: "Yeah."
>
> The flood waters had been more than eight feet high here. Every tree, blade of grass, and stray stick had its flood mark; cakey, yellow mud. It clung to the ground, cracking thinly here and there in spider web fashion. Over the stark fields came a gusty spring wind. . . . Over all hung a first-day strangeness.[5]

Wright's image of "a first-day strangeness" captures the human experience of a once familiar place now emptied of the taken-for-granted; a place Alfred Schutz might recognize as one where "the accent of reality is withdrawn."[6] Consider these words from several Katrina survivors, each in her or his own way pointing to a space scraped clean of the commonplace:

"My stove floated into the living room."

"The sofa was on top of the refrigerator. That's not right."

"There on the corner, not fifty yards from my house, was an alligator."

"We lived for two years in a FEMA trailer, the three of us. Seventy-six square feet and nowhere to go."

"I just drove away from the house so I could cry. I couldn't let them see me cry."

"For about three or four days I had dreams about water, dreams about floating, dreams about flooding, and would wake up every morning staring at the ceiling thinking, 'Where am I and what a terrible dream that was.'"

At once a banker, violinist, and sociologist who barely escaped Austria on the eve of the Nazi occupation, perhaps Schutz had himself in mind when he wrote about the cascading effects of the unforeseen:

When experiences [that] disconfirm the validity of my life-world began to mount one after another the taken-for-granted nature of my experiences explodes. In this situation, I can no longer reason in the same way about the world.[7]

What happens when the mantras of daily life, the "this is patently obvious," the "I can always do it again," the "and so forth and so on"—the foundation of my commonplace—become meaningless words unable to tame the world before me? What happens when I can no longer reason in the same way about the world, but reason I must?

Pamela Harold, a longtime resident of the Hollygrove neighborhood, lights up this existential weirdness:

I used to drive to work, and I would end up at a house that was, literally, a neighborhood that was . . . And I'm going like, "What's wrong with me? I know this." You know, ... "Why did I come to this neighborhood?" You know, I got so used to going by Mom's. And I'm showing up going like, "Oh my God, something's wrong with me." It's scary when you think that you did that, you know. I'm like, "Ooh noooo." All I know is that I'm in automatic mode, and I'm going from day to day, and I have feelings that I don't have words to express.

The waters of Hurricane Katrina washed away or at the very least badly damaged those singular cognitive maps that served to guide people through the mazeway of the city. The immediate material world of house or apartment as well as the surrounding streets, intersections, and other familiar landmarks was now barely discernible. In short, that almost natural, largely unreflecting, commonsense world fashioned through the mundane thoughts and practices that make up people's daily rounds retreated with Katrina's waters. The cadence of the ordinary was withdrawn.

AND THE WATER CAME

I had a dream the night before the water came. In my dream I see both my parents, who have been dead for some time. And I see a good friend of theirs a little bit further up the street. Old Mr. George was his name. And I saw Mr. George, they was friends with my parents. But all of them are dead. I see them in my dream walking the neighborhood, and it was almost like they was warning you to get out. My parents and all their dead friends were just walking and telling me, you know, "You better go and get out." They were saying, "Just take one more look, one last look, because it's time to go."

DAVID SAWYER, PONTCHARTRAIN PARK

David dreamt of water in the relative safety of a hotel room miles away from his neighborhood. He and his family evacuated the city ahead of the flood. But many others did not or could not escape the water. Many lived with it and in it for several days. Their flood-level view brings us close to the unscripted craziness of life lived on the thin thread of happenstance.

On August 28, 2005, the front page of the New Orleans *Times-Picayune* spelled out in several-inch bold font a portent of things to come: "KATRINA TAKES AIM." A subtitle read, "Levees Could be Topped in the Entire Metro Area." By early Monday morning, August 30, the storm surge from Katrina's winds breached the levees protecting the city at more than fifty locations. In some places more than nine feet of brownish, foul-smelling water heaved over rooftops, leaving just ridges of pitched roofs visible from the air. Between four and nine feet of this stuff found its way to Hollygrove and Pontchartrain Park, submerging stop signs and mailboxes and reaching roof lines.

Most of New Orleans flooded slowly. Imagine a leak in the side of a child's plastic pool. The water escapes and spreads about the lawn, filling

1.2. An aerial photo of New Orleans, early September 2005, looking from north to south at the height of the flood. Photograph used with permission from the *Dallas Morning News*.

the low patches, reaching as far as its mass allows. At the site of the leak, the water pours out with more force but quickly loses momentum and simply fills up the space surrounding it, standing still until soaked up by the earth or evaporated by the sun. For some, the water appeared without warning.

Longtime Hollygrove residents Philip and Victoria Harrington, both in their early seventies at the time of the flood, recall the night this wicked visitor seeped in uninvited.

"I SWAM OVER AND GOT ON TOP OF THE CARPORT"

We were sitting down and my hand went like that and water was up there. The water started coming up through the floor and taking me and my wife. She started grabbing blankets to put down there. We were getting out of here; she was crying. She said, "Look, my chair is floating!" I said, "Let's float out of here. Don't worry about those chairs." My wife said, "Pray, pray." I said, "Prayer is alright but we better get out of here."

And get out they did.

My son Phil came; he made a raft. He tied the raft alongside the house and I told him, "Put your mother on there." She got on the raft. I tried to get on it and it began to sink. So I told Phil, "You take your mother out as far as you can." What I did then was swim. I swam over and got on top of the carport. I said, "I'll be here until you come back."

Seven decades and counting on life's journey, Mr. Harrington is swimming to reach his carport and live another day. The Harringtons managed to get out of the water and onto high ground at Carrollton Avenue, where they stayed for a day and a half before an Army truck picked them up.

We got on the Army truck and they said, "Well, we are taking y'all to the Saints [football] training camp." So, we are at the Saints training camp and they say, "Well, we don't have no room for you; we can't take you in." So we got on a bus and they say, "Well, we are sending y'all to LSU Baton Rouge." But the university in Baton Rouge can't take us. They've got no more room. So we went to different hotels around the area and they couldn't take us so we ended up in Denham Springs, Louisiana, in a huge gymnasium.

Like Philip Harrington, Ronald Sandman was more than seven decades old when Katrina's waters flooded Pontchartrain Park. Living alone, he made the decision to ride out the storm in his home on Congress Street. Ronald had a doctor's appointment the next day to have stitches removed from a nasty cut on his leg. He built a pallet to raise himself off the kitchen floor. He slept on it Sunday night. Monday morning he awoke to find water lapping at the top of his makeshift bed.

"I GOT UNDER THE WATER AND . . .
SWAM UNTIL I GRABBED THE PORCH"

I said, "Well, I have to get out of here." And truthfully, the water was rising fast. All of a sudden, it was going faster, higher and higher. I went toward the front door, but I couldn't get out the front door because the sofa and chairs blocked the door. But I always kept a set of keys there at the back door. And I said, "How am I going to get out of here?" The washer and dryer had blocked the back door. I was able to push stuff out of the way, and now I have to feel where the keys are, but I was able to open the door and the door was swollen, but I was able to pull the door open. So I just scooted and maneuvered because this leg wasn't working at all. And going out, when I got out the back door, I forgot about the step down, and that's when the water hit here. I said, "Oh my God." That water was chin high.

My truck was parked in the carport, and I just hopped around until I got there. My plan was to get on top of my truck. I figured I was safe getting on top of the truck, but I saw the water was coming. I realized the water was full-on, and sitting on that truck would be a no-no. Then I saw a little opening, a crack in the wall of the ceiling. I climbed through it.

Mr. Sandman spent more than two days wedged into a two-and-a-half-foot-high crawl space between the ceiling and roof of his carport. He does not remember tying the bag that contained his cell phone, a radio, and two bottles of water around his neck.

So I'm just there. But I can hear boats and I can hear people yelling and talking. I could see that the water reached all the way to the gutters. I'm afraid to move. I can hear the people in the boat pass by. The water is as high as I am. But I have to do something. I could sit up somewhat, but the heat coming from the roof was really getting me. The water was so high I thought, "Where am I going to go if I get out of here?" My leg was definitely hurting and I felt something, I thought it was stinging. The worms and the bugs had gotten to the leg, but I didn't realize it then because I was so miserable and hot. But something said to me, "You got to make a move."

The house behind me, they had a sun porch, and the sun porch had come loose. And with the helicopters flying over here going boom, boom, this porch comes floating right towards me. I said to myself, "I'm going."

"KATRINA TAKES AIM" **23**

So I got in the water and I just took a chance and swam until I grabbed the porch. I was able to maneuver myself to sit on it. Gradually I was able to kneel on it. I took my sweater or jacket or something, and I started waving it until a helicopter saw me.

The guy in the helicopter sent the basket down, and he's yelling at me to get into the basket. I couldn't put this bad leg in it, so I got one leg in and this leg was up, out here like that. And he's lifting me. I tilt over and down I went into the water. I was up above the house and hit the water; at least I missed hitting the house. I finally got in the helicopter, and he flew me to the lakefront and then to Causeway Boulevard.

Ronald Sandman was left on the street to fend for himself and tend his worm-infested leg. He was lying on the ground exhausted when two people walked up and gazed down at him. They recognized him from the neighborhood. To Mr. Sandman these two were strangers; but Mr. Sandman was not a stranger to them.

I was wet, I was cold, I was hungry, and so a couple came there and said, "Mr. Sandman, we know you." I didn't know them; they were strangers to me. The man said, "We are going to look out for you, you are sick." I was having chills and fever. And they called the paramedics and they came to check me over. They put me in the ambulance and said, "We are going to Baton Rouge." Those two people were also able to contact my son; and then they disappeared. I still don't know their names.

Happenstance is where you find it.

When he arrived in Baton Rouge at the medical staging area set up at the Pete Maravich Assembly Center, medical personnel cut his clothes off and examined his leg.

I am conscious. I can hear them, "Oh my God? Look at his leg!" And they had a little conference and they said, "He's going to lose that leg." I heard that. They said, "I think we have bad news. I think you are going to lose this leg." "Excuse me," I said, "get me out of this pain, take the motherfucking thing off." That's the way I felt about that. I just wanted to get out [of] this pain.

Man, I saw the leg. All them little critters. Swollen, the flesh is open and you could see some of the stitches and the clamps and the little nasty things crawling in my leg. That's a horrible thing to see, the maggots. Oh man, it was horrible. I told them, "Take the leg, please take the leg. Get me out of this pain and take the leg." I just felt like, if you take the leg, I'm going to live. You don't take the leg, I going to die. So take the leg.

The near hysteria of the moment gave way to a more considered examination of the bug-infested leg. The doctors decided to clean it up and save it. Mr. Sandman has his leg and with it an account of how disaster can, under the right circumstances, leave one at the mercy of floating porches, helicopters, people who happen to recognize you though you've no idea who they are, and physicians who choose to act with calm and deliberation in a protracted moment of confusion.

Violet Green was eighty-five years old when Katrina hit. She lived alone in Pontchartrain Park. She had weathered Hurricane Betsy in this house in 1965, and she thought Katrina "was just going to be a wind and some rain and some water and the next day the sun would be out and we'd be home." But Ms. Green had second thoughts about riding the storm out at home and alone. On Sunday she decided to go to a school on Canal Street where she was told people were taking refuge to wait out the hurricane.

"I'M GOING TO TAKE YOU ALL DOWN TO THE UNDERTAKER"

And when I got there, they said, "Oh, no, this is just temporary. We are just taking people from here to the Superdome." I wasn't about to go to the Dome. So a cab came up with some people and I asked the lady was she still working. She said, "You'll be my last load." So she brought me home.

But home was about to become a perilous place.

I heard things flying and falling and breaking, so the young man next door said, "Ms. Violet, you better get out that house by yourself and go next door by the neighbor's." So I went over there, knocked on the door, she said come on in. So we stayed and the water came. It began to rain. The wind was blowing. My neighbor's roof started leaking bad. So we came outside and stood in the gate. So my neighbor says, "You know, Ms. Ana Pearl left her key with us. That's the first time she ever did that. She said we might need it." Ms. Pearl has that upstairs across the street. So the young man, his mother and father and me, we decided to go over there.

The next morning, I didn't look out the window. I just went to the door to go down the stair steps, and by the time I hit first top step, I stepped in water. From upstairs, up there, I stepped in water! And I looked down and there was a refrigerator and tables and chairs and everything floating. I couldn't believe what I was seeing. I said, "Oh my God, I wonder if we'll ever get out of here." And the other lady, she was my neighbor, she was a diabetic and she was really very upset.

They had some young men in boats trying to help get people out of here, and we were in the window waving pillow slips or whatever we could find to let them know we were there. And after a while a young man came and got us and we had to get out of the window and get on top of the carport.

So I am eighty-five and she is diabetic. Whew! The boat, it took us out to the Chef [Highway]. So we went to the shopping center and everybody was just in a daze or something. We just sat around and walked around and looked around. Then somebody had a smart idea. All of us neighbors who lived together, knew each other, we wanted to stick together. So this young man said, "I'll tell you what, you older people, I'm going to take you all down to the undertaker and we're going to stay there."

So we went to the undertaker's, the funeral home, and it was late, it was getting dark. No lights or nothing, so the young men went to the grocery store. They got candles for lights. Our group stayed together, and when daylight came they went to the grocery store for us and they got us groceries.[8]

We stayed at the undertakers for three or four days before a chopper came down low enough and he saw us. He asked us, "There are people staying in the funeral home?" We said, "Yes, live people, we are all alive." They decided to take us to the airport. We got to the airport, it was jammed. They had one young man, he stayed with us. He said, "Mama Violet, I'm going to stick with you." So they let him get on a plane with me and we ended up in Corpus Christi, Texas. You didn't know where you are going until you got on the plane.

After sleeping with the dead for several nights, this elderly woman finds herself in Texas. And her journey has just begun. If the deep meaning of chance and strangeness needed a case in point, Ms. Green's experiences would serve with emphasis.

Joseph Pratt is a retired postal truck driver who was born and raised around Forshey Street in Hollygrove. He grew up rough in this working-class neighborhood; it probably came as no surprise to his daughter when he ignored her plea to evacuate. "No thank you," he said politely, "I always just stick it out."

"HE DIDN'T MAKE IT. HE WOUND UP DYING, MAN"

I was real tired; I remember I laid down with my work clothes on. So, roundabout I'd say about 12 o'clock, 12:30 that night I had fell asleep. I heard the wind whistling, it's making a "oooohhh" . . . and that's what woke me up. And I can just hear the wind blowing. I said, "Oh this might be a bad one here." I remember the window on the side of the house crashed, boom. I got up and lit me a candle, but when the window broke out, all the wind was blowing in and it was so dark and all the drapes were blowing. I said, "Man, I gotta get out of this front room and I'm a go all the way to the back room." So I went and got in the back bed. I went back to sleep I was so tired.

I brought the puppy and I put him in the bed with me, and being up laying in the bed, I fell off to sleep again and subconsciously I woke up and I looked—I had a candle lit in the bedroom, I looked down at the floor and I could see from the candle the water had got into the house, and I said, "Man, this must be going to be bad because we never experience water back here in this neighborhood." And at that point I got up out the bed and I went up in the attic—opened up the attic and I went up there, me and the puppy. I laid down up there. I went back to sleep. So around about 5:30–6 o'clock daylight was breaking, I look out . . . I can see daylight through the planks in the attic and I came back downstairs, I came down through the water. I say maybe about four or five feet of water at that time. I came out the house, me and the puppy, I went in the backyard and I got my boat. I had a flat boat back then. The water was four or five feet high in the backyard. I tied the boat to a fence.

I walked through the water, and I got in the boat and all I could hear people across the street, "Come get me," all the people standing up over in the upstairs house over there, and they got up because they couldn't get through the water, some of them . . . some of them folks was higher up . . . you talking about five feet, it was almost over their kids' heads. So immediately I went over there and I started getting people at that point and bringing them up to where they was evacuating people up on Claiborne and Monticello Avenue.

So it was for Mr. Pratt, who spent a week in the brutal heat and fetid water pulling his neighbors from the flood and transporting them to higher ground. But he could not save everyone.

People died from around the neighborhood. Some of my best buddies, man! I don't know how they went to sleep—I think they had been drinking or something and they wind up falling asleep over there, three of them in a house on Olive Street. The water got up in the house over there real bad and wind up drowning all of them.

People were dying. It was ugly. One guy, he sat in the red ants, and the red ants ate him up out there on Claiborne and Monticello. He couldn't get away from them red ants for nothing, man. He must have had a billion red ants all over him. A few days later I asked about him. They told me died at Ochsner [Hospital]. I think due to an infection in his body. He didn't make it; he was another one dead.

We were sleeping out there on the high ground at Claiborne and Monticello Avenue. I found an old garbage truck to sleep in. One morning I got out the garbage truck, looked like my legs had swelled or something from being in that water.

We'd been there about a week or more and the police told us to get out because the water had got so bad. They didn't know if they had enough medicine to protect people from the bad water. One of the evacuation trucks was sitting there empty. I told the police I was about to start the truck up, could I take it? The policeman told me if I could start the truck up, take it. So I broke in the truck and broke the switch out. It was a stake-body truck and it had two gas tanks on it, diesel tanks. So I found a hose pipe, siphoned the gas out the garbage truck I was sleeping in, and filled both of my tanks up on the stake-body truck. I told all those that wanted to go I could drop them off in Baton Rouge.

Here I am driving a truck I broke into. I've got no driver's license because my wallet was in the cabinet here at home. But the New Orleans police told me just tell anyone who might stop me as I was going up there what the situation was and it would be alright. I'm glad I didn't get stopped.

Like Lévi-Strauss's *bricoleur*, Mr. Pratt cobbles together what is at hand to effect survival for him and many others, lighting up the resourcefulness born from a blue-collar life.[9]

IF WATER REMEMBERED

If water had a memory it might well have felt it was returning home that day late in August 2005 as it filled the topographical bowl that is New Orleans. Those first French explorers who set foot on what is now the southern edge of the Vieux Carré, the French Quarter, knew for all practical purposes that they were standing on an island. For two weeks following the unprecedented flood of 2005, the Quarter stood once again high and dry while water lapped at its edge. One could, if so inclined, motor a boat from this edge to Lake Pontchartrain, the entire length of the city. For the better part of two weeks the Quarter stood as a reminder to those who care about such things that a few feet in elevation made the difference between being in and out of water.

The water came as if determined to reclaim its lost home. People caught in it lived on the edge, literally and figuratively. They pushed their often damaged bodies into attics, out of windows, and through the russet, stinky water itself. They sought what high ground they could, from a garbage truck to a funeral home. The force of logical argument cannot "explain" life in the water. Mr. and Mrs. Harrington, Mr. Sandman, Ms. Green, Mr. Pratt, and the tens of thousands of others were forced to make their own islands in the hopes of living another day. But rivaling, if not trumping, the inanity of those days is the plain fact that none of this should have happened in the first place.

"HURRICANE PAM," A DEVASTATING FANTASY

Well before the terrorist attacks of 9/11, FEMA had identified the three most likely catastrophic events to occur in the United States: a hurricane and storm surge striking New Orleans and the Gulf Coast, a major earthquake on the U.S. West Coast, and a terrorist attack on New York City.[10] This was, in hindsight, a prescient assessment of impending danger. Based on its risk projection, FEMA began preparing for a worst-case disaster in New Orleans and several parishes in Louisiana. The agency simulated a hurricane coming ashore on the southern edge of the state. "Hurricane Pam" was a devastating fantasy.

This virtual hurricane struck New Orleans in July 2004. Packing sustained winds of 120 miles per hour, Pam dropped up to twenty inches of rain on southeastern Louisiana. Its storm surge topped the levees at New Orleans. More than a million people were evacuated, and more than 500,000 buildings were destroyed.[11] An elaborate simulation, on the one hand, a portent of things to come on the other. Hurricane Pam was "designed to be the first step toward producing a comprehensive hurricane response plan, jointly approved and implemented by federal, state and city officials."[12]

Reflecting on the Hurricane Pam simulation sometime after Katrina struck New Orleans, Walter Maestri, the emergency manager and Homeland Security coordinator for Jefferson Parish, which overlaps Orleans Parish, said simply, "Everything that happened in Pam, which was an exercise, happened in Katrina. And that's what perplexes me . . . because FEMA also participated in that exercise."[13]

FEMA Director Michael Brown would later admit that the agency did not have the funding to put into place what participants had learned from this elaborate rehearsal.[14] Recently moved into the Department of Homeland Security, its budget slashed to increase funding for the "war on terror," FEMA was not equipped to manage the chaos that was Miss Katrina. The hurricane, by all accounts, was more fearsome than FEMA was organized. From the vantage point of several years after the wind, the failed levees, and the flooding of the city, it is fair to say that Hurricane Katrina was one of those flawless federal failures, a protracted moment in which nature erupted and government agencies too small and underfunded flailed about in efforts to help.

The disconnect between this historic hurricane and the federal risk assessment pointing to it is nicely captured in remarks made by the chief executive of the United States on September 1, 2005. Making his first public statement about the storm, President George W. Bush stated emphatically—without a hint of awareness that Hurricane Pam had foretold Katrina—"I don't think anybody anticipated the breach of the levees in New Orleans."[15] He was dead wrong.[16]

ANTICIPATING THE NEXT CHAPTER

The rule of contingency and chance is the magnetic north of this book; it will pull our gaze in its direction time and time again. But there are moments throughout when we deliberately focus on the relation of happenstance with the vicissitudes of material well-being. That class and the unforeseen are somehow connected should not surprise us. How they are coupled is a second theme of this book. In the next chapter we introduce this theme in the context of two historic New Orleans neighborhoods.

2

GEOGRAPHIES OF CLASS AND COLOR

Perhaps more than any city its size, New Orleans is a patchwork of neighborhoods, or faubourgs, each with a heritage and identity that sets it off from the others. The parish of Orleans is a collage of seventeen wards containing no less than seventy-two neighborhoods. Names like Treme, Marigny, and St. Roch reflect the city's French heritage, while Lakeshore, Lakeview, and Lake Vista signal the white flight and suburban expansion of the city into the swamps and reclaimed land on the shores of Lake Pontchartrain beginning in the late 1930s. The English already had settled in the Garden District and Uptown, while Irish immigrants clustered in what to this day is called the Irish Channel. If the borders between neighborhoods are not obvious to strangers, they assume a purpose and meaning for those who call New Orleans home.

If I know that someone lives in Faubourg St. John, for example, I am also likely to know that there are roughly as many African Americans living in the neighborhood as whites, with a sprinkling of people from Latin American countries. I also know a bit about residential segregation by race and class. That part of the neighborhood on the river side of Bayou St. John above Dumaine Street is nearly all black and working class, while that part of the neighborhood on the lake side of the bayou is nearly all white and middle class. Regardless of the side of the bayou on which one resides, most everyone in this neighborhood counts the annual Endymion Parade among their favorite Mardi Gras moments; all eyes are on the Olympian God and his entourage as it rolls right through the heart of this faubourg.

Hollygrove and Pontchartrain Park each has its own distinct story about race and class. Diverse housing styles, demographics, and cultures reflect these differences. Hollygrove is in the Seventeenth Ward, a district that includes the Leonidas and Dixon neighborhoods, among others. The neighborhood is mostly black; some people are poor, most are working class, and a few are middle-class professionals.

Hollygrove took on the character of a neighborhood during the 1920s as marshland was drained to build houses. At the turn of the twenty-first century, the average household income in Hollygrove was just over $30,000 per year, and more than 28 percent of all households subsisted below the official poverty level.[1]

One way of discerning the class background of a New Orleans neighborhood is to identify the entertainers who grew up in that place. With Hollygrove's deep connection to manual labor and a working-class culture, it is not surprising to find a number of noted rap artists who were raised in Hollygrove, among them Fiend, Mack Maine, and Lil' Wayne. Noted R&B singer the late Johnny Adams also hails from Hollygrove. The pop and roots music of the neighborhood echoes the stamp of blue-collar black culture on this urban plat.

By contrast, Pontchartrain Park is a historically middle-class enclave within New Orleans' Second Ward, which stretches from the Mississippi River to Lake Pontchartrain. Pontchartrain Park originated as a planned subdivision for upwardly mobile African American families. Here live schoolteachers, postal workers, professors, engineers, and computer programmers. In 2000 the average annual household income in this housing tract was $44,000, not quite 50 percent higher than the middling income of Hollygrove households. The number of households below the poverty level in Pontchartrain Park in 2000 stood at 10 percent.[2]

If Hollygrove nurtured rap artists and soul singers, among the entertainers who called Pontchartrain Park home are Grammy Award–winning jazz trumpeter Terence Blanchard and actor Wendell Pierce, from HBO's *The Wire* and *Treme*. Lisa Perez Jackson, former chief of the U.S. Environmental Protection Agency, also grew up in Pontchartrain Park. So did Ernest "Dutch" Morial, the first black mayor of New Orleans, and his son, Mark, who also served two terms as mayor and is now president of the National Urban League.

It is worth noting, however, that although the two neighborhoods represent a distinction between working and middle classes, there are individuals and families in each neighborhood who belie a too-strict division between the two enclaves. It is the nature of market economies, Terry Eagleton notes, to "confound distinctions . . . and mix the most diverse forms of life promiscuously together."[3] Class in situ is messier than class in abstraction. Some of the people we interviewed in Hollygrove are closer to the middle than to the working class, and a few of those in Pontchartrain Park live much like people do in Hollygrove.

With this caveat in mind, to say to oneself and others "I live in Pontchartrain Park" is to lay claim to a place and an identity that differs in important ways from that person who says "I live in Hollygrove." Howard Rodin grew up in Hollygrove and now lives next door to Pontchartrain Park. Describing the differences between the two neighborhoods, he draws a sharp contrast: "Hollygrove is family and politics, while Pontchartrain Park is upscale, wide-open spaces, the golf course." Those differences help us make some sense of both the number and kind of contingencies people encountered in the aftermath of Katrina and how they responded to them.

While it is too much to say that the residents of Hollygrove and Pontchartrain Park experienced different disasters, there are nevertheless subtle and not-so-subtle differences in their lived experiences of this historic flood, and these differences are connected to the alternating fortunes of material well-being.[4]

In the most ordinary of times, class is more than an apparition that floats just outside our web of life; on the contrary, our day-to-day struggles, routines, or what counts as the ordinary are laced with the durable twine of social class.[5] Perhaps there are some protected spaces immune from the elastic reach of capital, but surely the difficult work of remaking a commonplace world following a catastrophic flood, of salvaging some sense of humanness from the material, psychological, and social debris left afterward, is joined in some discernible ways with the limitations and possibilities of class. It should come as no surprise that in those most uncommon moments of our lives, when we are called to muster what resources we can, both personal and material, the advantages that stem from class can make a real difference.

In sum, we expected the stories we were told to vary somewhat by the conditions that class creates. It would be misleading, however, to say that differences in material circumstances explain all or most of the variance found in the accounts we collected in Hollygrove and Pontchartrain Park; but to put social class on the table, examine it, and then wipe it off leaves just the hint of truth the idea warrants. With this trace of truth in mind, we juxtapose narratives now and then to illustrate the ways in which differences in material circumstances shape the stories we heard. Consider these two brief quotes, one from Clara Carrington of Pontchartrain Park and the other from Jerry Wright of Hollygrove.

Clara recalls:

My husband is from Florida, a little town called Crescent City, Florida. And we have a lot of property and land there. So I said, let's just go there. In the meantime a very close friend of ours called us and said he had a house that was available, a nice-size house that we could bring the whole family there. And it was ready and waiting for us.

Jerry remembers trying to wait out the water for five days before walking

to the causeway because we seen helicopters kept passing. So we just figured out that's where they were going, picking up people and stuff. So we just walked over there. They had a lot of people. They had shuttle buses for taking people out of New Orleans, and they brought us to Thibodaux to Nichols State, the college . . . And we were there for a couple of hours until some other people came and asked if we wanted to go to New Iberia. We didn't really have a plan.

Clara is a middle-class professional woman in her early seventies. Jerry is a young man in his twenties from a working-class family; he was working odd jobs and considering trade school when Katrina struck. Embedded in these two brief descriptions of life shortly after the city flooded is a simple but compelling idea: there will be moments in disaster when choices and contingencies are shaped directly by material and social well-being, a relative sum. The concrete work of surviving disaster, in other words, is partly an artifact of the stubborn and limiting constraints of material accumulation.

But lest we leave the impression that the working class is always at a disadvantage relative to the middle class, there are times, as we will see, when simply being working-class can shape expectations in ways that preclude the middle-class inclination to be both surprised and angry when government fails to act in a humane and timely manner. In the previous chapter, Joseph Pratt, a lifelong resident of Hollygrove and jack-of-all-trades recounts how he hotwired a truck, siphoned gas, and drove himself and others to Baton Rouge and out of harm's way. These are working-class skills. In addition to knowing something about cars and trucks, blue-collar workers often possess at least a few of the skills needed to rebuild a damaged house. Perhaps one person has a skill, say, at electricity, and the neighbor next door knows plumbing, inviting a swap of needed talents.

So, we should not be surprised when differences in material well-being show up now and then to help us account for the sometimes dramatic variations in how this disaster was experienced. But the fortunes of class are more often than not eclipsed by the unrelenting play of happenstance. It is the mutable and awkward dance between the two that we aim to capture in this story. It is time now to take a brief tour of these two neighborhoods.

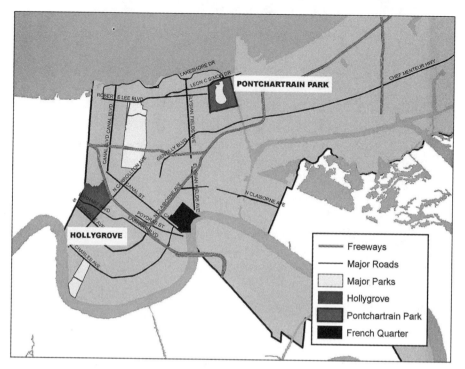

2.1. The Hollygrove and Pontchartrain Park neighborhoods, New Orleans. Map by Carrie Beth Lasley, Wayne State University.

HOLLYGROVE

We begin with a short ride back in time, before August 2005. We'll start our trip with a visit to Hollygrove. It's best to ride with someone who knows the city; driving around in it may be likened to a sight-impaired rodent navigating a maze. There are roads in New Orleans that lead nowhere, roads that end abruptly at a bayou, canal, or railroad track. A person can lose her way here as the city bends and curves to accommodate the river and canals. We drive down Carrollton Avenue, one of the main thoroughfares in New Orleans that more or less traverses the western edge of the city from north to south, from City Park to the Mississippi River (figure 2.1).

We descend from what the locals call "high ground"—two to four feet above sea level—near City Park. We pass raised houses where two ridges meet, a topography created by silt deposited from two long-defunct tributaries of the Mississippi River. We make an imperceptible descent to the place where Interstate 10 crosses Carrollton and forms the northern bound-

2.2. Hollygrove Street sign. Photo by Emma Kroll-Smith.

ary of Hollygrove. We are now once again below sea level, in what locals call the "black city," where the attendant at the self-service gas station sits behind a wire cage with a little slot at the bottom for money to change hands. The land that Hollygrove sits on ranges in elevation from two to four feet below sea level.[6]

Originally bought from plantation owners by speculators whose money was also tied up in the slave trade, the beginning of this faubourg foreshadowed the story of race and racism that is one of its dominant narratives. Every modern race story can be found here: segregation, integration, white flight, redlining, the decline of public schools, businesses that abandon the area, and the rampage of drugs and violence in inner-city neighborhoods.

A street sign tells us we have entered Hollygrove. Dotting the landscape is the occasional pothole, an abandoned house, young men in low-slung pants and hats askew standing on street corners, and properly dressed grandmothers sitting on their front porches. The neighborhood's architecture is a mad mix of styles. A Creole cottage may sit next to a slab-on-grade brick ranch-style house next to a shotgun house—a narrow house, often no more than a twelve feet wide, with rooms arranged one behind the other and bookended by front and back doors. A few houses have been added onto so many times that it is hard to tell where their original foundations lay.

The layout of the neighborhood tells a complicated story. It emerged piecemeal, with no forethought, from residual land left over from the planned neighborhoods that surround it. Hollygrove is, to put it plainly, an accidental neighborhood. If you attempt to navigate it, the phrase "carefully designed" is not likely to come to mind. The neighborhood is dissected by two major overpass roads, Earhart Expressway and Airline Highway. At street level, it is crossed by several rail lines and canals. A drive from one side to the other requires getting on and off a major highway and weaving one's way over bridges and around dead-end streets. Neighborhood historian Kylee Grimm describes the physical contours of Hollygrove this way:

> The things that dissect or cut Hollygrove up are the canal, the highway, Earhart Expressway, Carrollton Avenue. When you come along with the concepts of census tracks, then it gets cut up kind of interestingly. My understanding is they were having a meeting one night and someone says, "Well, let's call this patch Hollygrove-Dixon" because they wanted

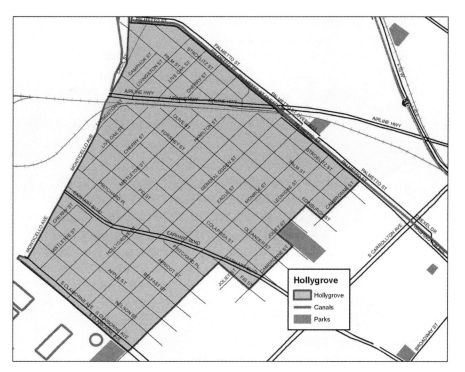

2.3. Grid map of Hollygrove. By Carrie Beth Lasley, Wayne State University.

to distinguish it from Hollygrove across the highway. I like to be a Hollygrove purist because when Mama first started living here, there was no Airline Highway, there was no canal, there was no overpass. It used to be you could just drive across on these streets because we were all one neighborhood.

Ms. Grimm could be channeling urban historian Lewis Mumford, who himself might just as well have been writing about Hollygrove when he described the unplanned consequences of spatial advance in a market economy:

> The town itself consisted of the shattered fragments of land, with odd shapes and inconsequential streets and avenues, left over between the factories, the railroads, the freight yards and the dump heaps.[7]

The transected nature of Hollygrove is visually represented in the photo of Miss Harold's day care center, stuffed hard between the Palmetto Canal and Earhart Expressway.

Like most of New Orleans, Hollygrove was once swamp. It was gradually drained and turned into farmland. After World War I, a few black families settled in this soggy bottomland, clustered in housing separate from their white working-class counterparts. Farmland slowly changed into plots for houses inhabited by black and white laborers and craftsmen who worked on the docks and in the sugar industry, while women were commonly employed as domestics in the homes of the wealthy. Scattered in present-day Hollygrove are the descendants of these black maids and laborers. Philip Harrington, a retired Chevron worker whose family members were among the first African Americans to settle in what is now Hollygrove, takes us back to a time when much of the area was still swampland:

> My grandfather said when he was building that house it was nothing but swampland. They had to float the wood and lumber back in there to build on South Murat Street at that time. They had to get the wood back there on mules and put some of the wood in canoes to bring it back to the house.

Kylee Grimm tells a story about how her grandparents were able to buy a lot, and over time and aided by family and neighbors, they built their house in Hollygrove.

> They acquired this lot in 1937, and it took them ten years to pay it off. Now we are talking $750; and when you break that down it's like maybe six dollars and something a month, and you might have to break that

2.4. Miss Pamela Harold's day care center, beyond the overpass and canal, in Hollygrove. Photo by Amanda Figueroa.

down into a weekly amount. So they paid a few dollars every week for ten years for the lot. After they acquired the lot, their largest expense was building materials because as far as labor goes, people really helped you build the house.

Prior to the 1960s, Hollygrove was working-class in the traditional New Orleans style. A few blocks of all-white households sat next to a few blocks of all-black households, creating a salt-and-pepper quilt pattern in the neighborhood. Evelyn Wright remembers the supportive family atmosphere growing up in the 1940s:

Oh, in those days it was nice, it was nice over there. We had a big old lot there that you could go play ball in and everything right across the street from your house. When it was time for you to go in, Daddy would give you that whistle and you knew it was time to go home. But it was fun then. Children don't do the stuff we used to do. Yep, playing ball, shooting marbles, and all of that, they don't do those kinds of things anymore.

Diana Woodman remembers an interconnected network of families that looked after each other:

When I grew up there were a lot of connections here. We lived on one side; my cousin lived on the other side. Across the street another cousin grew up. Across the street from me there was this elderly lady. Her niece grew up down the street, and her niece's children went to school with me. There were two families with the same last name, like two brothers lived next door to each other. All of their siblings or relatives lived in other parts of the neighborhood. So there was a lot of connection in this neighborhood.

Many of those family connections Diana describes remain. But during the turbulent decade of the 1960s, school desegregation and white flight to the suburbs prompted the de facto segregation that continues to mark America's cities. Hollygrove became almost exclusively black and increasingly poor. Renters and those with marginal incomes found their way into the neighborhood. Howard Rodin remembers the demographic forces set in motion during those years, and he connects them to Hurricane Katrina:

After white flight, Palm Street changed from basically all white to African American. But the people who bought those houses maintained them and kept them up. Now Olive Street was a mixed neighborhood. When I was coming up, even though Monroe was like the dividing line, you had whites on this side, blacks on this side. Olive Street was still a somewhat mixed neighborhood. But as the years went on and white flight began, instead of selling those houses, they [departing whites] rented them. Now you had people who had bought their houses in between renters. One house here, one house there, but the majority, of course, were rentals. And so you start to see a decline in the neighborhood. And that was the problem all throughout Hollygrove, and you still have a lot of people who own their homes, and those are the ones you see putting their houses back up after Katrina. That's why the family aspect is so important here.

Jesse Gray augments Howard's more analytic account with a personal, up-close recollection of the changes he has experienced in Hollygrove:

We had some woods. There was a pond. Most everything back then was nothing but trees, open fields, cornfields, you know. And I always was an outdoors man. Then in the '60s came the drug-infested neighborhoods. Killings, burglarizing, a lot of strange people in the neighborhood.

Lifelong Hollygrove resident Evelyn Wright notes that changes in the neighborhood have been hardest on the young:

So many youngsters come up, you know, in the neighborhood. The crime and the dope and all of that, we never had to live like that, you know, boys hanging on the corner selling drugs. Things like that, you know, or somebody getting shot in the neighborhood. But all in all . . . this is my neighborhood. And I am not running from it; but it's all over, all over the neighborhood.

Stable networks of nuclear and extended families of working-class homeowners in Hollygrove now live side by side with less stable blended and extended families for whom steady work is scarce and the violence of the drug trade or drug use is always nearby.

PONTCHARTRAIN PARK

Okay, it is time to move on. We drive out of Hollygrove and head east for five miles. On the way we pass City Park and the University of New Orleans, go under several overpasses, and take a right onto Press Drive. On Press we drive into Pontchartrain Park. A planned middle-class black suburban housing tract, the Park is the second-oldest African American neighborhood in the United States, designed, as the local paper noted more than a half century ago, "for the wealthier Negro families."[8] A neat wrought-iron sign welcomes us to this neighborhood.

Like Hollygrove, this faubourg sits a couple of feet below sea level. If Hollygrove is a haphazard maze of streets and crisscrossed by canals and train tracks, Pontchartrain Park is divided, suburban-style, by a semicircle drive around a golf course. Streets branch off this half circle in the direction of the Industrial Canal and toward another housing section nestled behind the Southern University of New Orleans campus, built in the late 1950s. The houses reflect a mid-twentieth-century suburban motif: slab on grade, brick, small or nonexistent front porch, and a good-size front lawn. There is a properness connected to a sameness about this neighborhood. It is relatively safe from crime, lawns are fastidiously kept, fathers and mothers work, and children go to college.

Pontchartrain Park was built as an effort to appease a growing black middle class that was finding its political voice in opposition to segregation. Powerful whites reasoned that they could better maintain segregation across the city if they surrendered a sizable piece of valuable real estate to this emerging professional class of African Americans who could, in their segregated neighborhood, live the American Dream.

Then New Orleans Mayor deLesseps Story Morrison acknowledged the growing power of upwardly mobile African Americans and the 1950s challenge to the long-standing "separate but equal" race policy. "If we are going to preserve the traditions and the habits of our city, including seg-

2.5. Entrance to Pontchartrain Park subdivision. Photo by Emma Kroll-Smith.

regation," he declared, "we are going to have to provide facilities to meet the demands of the Negro people."[9] He meant, of course, that times were changing. America was moving in fits and starts away from segregation toward integration.[10] New Orleans would be wise to make some limited accommodation. Building separate but equal suburban developments to house middle-class blacks and whites was arguably the least damaging accommodation to the "traditions and habits of our city." A recent history of the neighborhood begins this way:

> In 1951, Pontchartrain Park was designed "for negroes" as a 190-acre recreation area with an 18-hole golf course, clubhouse, stadium, ball fields, basketball and tennis courts, playgrounds, picnic areas, and fishing lagoons—and as a 175-acre residential subdivision of 1,000 single-family homes.[11]

One hundred planned houses were sold in Pontchartrain Park before ground was broken, and by May 1958 more than 560 homes dotted the landscape.[12] Early residents were doctors, educators, ministers, contractors, postal workers, and young politicians like future mayor Ernest Morial. The city leadership planned this neighborhood with distinct borders so that it would not encroach on the white Gentilly Woods subdivision developed next door. To minimize the commingling of black and white, for years there was only one thoroughfare in and out of Pontchartrain Park.

In recent decades, as children grew up and moved out, the population of Pontchartrain Park aged. Thirty-four percent of the residents were over sixty-five in 2000, five years before the flood.[13] Howard Rodin draws a telling comparison between growing old in Hollygrove and in Pontchartrain Park:

> Now remember I said a lot of people in Hollygrove own their own homes. The second part of it is that their second generation stayed with them, extended family, so they were there to help them. Now, Pontchartrain Park before the storm had the largest elderly population in the city of New Orleans. These were concentrated elderly because Pontchartrain Park was settled in 1955. So a person in their twenties or thirties buys a house, moves into Pontchartrain Park, like my father. In the '50s, they are in their thirties, two young sons, they move into Pontchartrain Park. They put their kids in grammar school and high school. Those kids left. They got their degrees, some of them might have stayed in New Orleans, but if they did stay in New Orleans they moved into New Orleans East.

2.6. Grid map of Pontchartrain Park. By Carrie Beth Lasley, Wayne State University.

2.7. Opening of Pontchartrain Park, 1950s. Photo used with permission of the *Times-Picayune*.

Thomas Perkins Sr. is a good example. One of his sons, Tom Jr., grew up in Pontchartrain Park but got his degree in Baton Rouge and then moved from Baton Rouge to Dallas. One of the senior Mr. Perkins' daughters, she left and is living in Baltimore. Another son left the neighborhood to get his degree, and he is living in Minnesota. So now it's just Mr. and Mrs. Perkins left in the Park. Mr. Perkins Sr. died about 2003. So now it's just the mama there when the storm comes along.

By August 2005, Pontchartrain Park was no longer your grandmother's "hope of New Orleans." But the idea, of this planned neighborhood as a testament to the success of those African Americans who battled racism to achieve the middle-class American Dream, survived—and would survive the flood.

RACE AND WATER

The histories of Hollygrove and Pontchartrain Park, like all neighborhoods in New Orleans, are rooted in the complexities and conundrums of race and class. In modern America, the distinction between these two iconic words is notoriously leaky, though it is one worth making. When we began the research for this book we wondered what importance class and race differences might have in making sense of the stories we were told. At first we thought race might trump the marked socioeconomic differences between these working-class and middle-class African American neighborhoods, creating more continuities than differences in the stories we collected. We do find some persistent connections between the idea of race and people's personal experiences of Hurricane Katrina, but they are related more to an African American culture shared across class lines than to conscious efforts to frame the lived experiences of remaking a postdisaster world in racial terms.

When people narrate the disaster in the vocabulary of race, they do not refer to their personal experiences of the flood and its aftermath; rather they speak broadly of the history of racial oppression as a means for understanding why the government failed to act in a timely manner in the midst of a human catastrophe. Marie Saunders, a single woman who lives and operates a day care center in Hollygrove, talks about race and response to the storm in this way:

> The way Katrina happened I'm thinking had something to do with race, the way it was handled. You know, I mean that's my way of thinking. That's the way I look at it. I think things could have been handled much different. And it should have been handled different. You know it's happened for years and it continues to happen. But I think, had it been different, help probably would have been there faster, because we've gotten things to other countries faster. This is the United States!

Ms. Saunders grew up in a small town in central Louisiana at a time when black people were still at day-to-day risk from whites bent on violence. Deep in her bones she knows race still matters.

Michael Carrington, from Pontchartrain Park, frames the question of race in the marked differences between black and white interpretations of the government response to the hurricane:

> I think if you ask black people, by and large, they would say race was a factor in . . . the storm. If you ask whites, by and large, they would say it shouldn't have anything to do with race. I think in a way that's two different answers to the same question. Personally, I think it suggests that we haven't gotten that far in our race relations in this country.

Marie and Michael make sense of Katrina and the waters she troubled in ways that mirror the national discourse on this disaster. The images of black bodies floating in the fetid water, of chaos at the Superdome, of hundreds of African Americans stranded on highway overpasses for days with little water or food, all scream to the world America's historical dilemma in this epic failure of U.S. emergency response. For a few days in late August and early September 2005, racism was once again a nationwide matter.

In good times and bad, racism in New Orleans is akin to the heavy, miasmic air that lies like a damp cloth over the face of the city. It mingles with the oxygen. It's part of the cellular life of New Orleans. Perhaps it is this organic nature of racism that makes it an assumed but noiseless part of the many and varied stories we were told. Perhaps it is because we are white and the residents of both neighborhoods are black that it is considered indelicate to bring up racism in mixed-color conversation. We've no firm opinions about either of these possibilities, though we are inclined toward the first.

What we do know is that when people talked with us about this disaster, they laughed, cried, openly admitted their fears, expressed a visceral anger with this or that government program, took time to philosophize about its meaning for them personally and the world at large, and spoke all this with only an occasional reference to race or racism. In the end, we don't know whether race was a reflexive part of the stories people told us; what we do know is that they opened their hearts and minds to make some sense of the almost ineffable.

LOOKING FORWARD, TELLING ABOUT DISASTER

Parts II and III follow the lives of residents from both neighborhoods as they begin the long slog from evacuation to exile to seeking disaster assistance to rebuilding and the struggle to refashion a semblance of the ordinary. Departing from the normal social-science study of disaster, we will not ask anyone to confirm or disprove or to argue for or against anything in particular, in part because we won't produce anything like a fixed position so much as a series of positionings. Far from writing an orderly arrangement of things, our tale is one of muddle and confusion, arguably the true lords of life in the wake of catastrophe.

In dozens of conversations over the years we were struck by the unique story each person told of being tossed out of the familiar only to land in a shape-shifting space with little that appeared obvious or predictable. T. S. Eliot thought "Humankind" unable to "bear very much reality."[14] But Eliot likely never read the blow-by-blow accounts of people forced to push back hour by hour, day by day against the brute fact that their lives as they knew them were over. Here, standing unadulterated, is "very much reality" indeed. Everyone who spoke with us lived for months on the high wire of chance and serendipity; many lived there for years, and some might still be said to be struggling to remain balanced.

Each person we interviewed was faced with cobbling together a biographical solution to the many and varied contradictions forced on him or her by the confluence of an all-encompassing catastrophe and a woefully inadequate state and federal response. This formless moment, extending no one knows how far into the future, triggered a range of physical and psychological problems. For some, extreme and protracted stress compromised their physical health; others found themselves in the grip of mental and emotional troubles and wounds of a sort to psyches tossed about in Katrina's wake.

If we were struck by anything in our conversations with people in both neighborhoods it was their capacity to narrow their focus of attention to the details of survival. If there is one theme common to all the stories we recorded it is the way Hurricane Katrina opened a lingering moment in which each life was lived on a scheme of uncertified possibilities. When all is said and done, however, as these stories reveal, it is not chance or contingency that mattered most; it is what people did when they came face to face with bewildering uncertainty that is the heart of the issue. Reason or sense-making, Geertz reminds us, is not something the things or events of the world give to us; it is rather a quality that we bestow on those things and events, however chaotic.[15]

Telling about themselves, the hurricane, the flood, the chaotic relief efforts, and so on did not appear to be a chore.[16] Some told their stories as a kind of lament; their words had the sound of sighs strung together into narrative. At other times the story was told at the pitch of passion, words tumbling upon words, a trail of feelings from beginning to end. Still others narrated their accounts in a methodical and matter-of-fact cadence, moving from one untoward moment to the next. However the story was told, it was in the telling that the teller was making something meaningful out of the outright overwhelming.

The practical result of presenting a wide sampling of voices is to give our story a weight no logical argument could match for immediacy, intensity, and range of experience. Our intent was to assemble a mass of testimony not easily talked down by or gathered up into general propositions. We leave room for you, the reader, to find your own meanings in these narratives, to draw your own conclusions. But if we've done our job as we intended to do it, as you read these first-person narratives, it should, to borrow a line from William Labov, "be unthinkable for you to say 'So what?'"[17]

Together these hundreds of transcribed pages scattered about our desks recall a note from Michael Roemer, who reminds us that the hero in story and drama "is obliged to take upon himself a task the community cannot carry out."[18] The strong connection between the literary hero going it alone in the absence of civic support, indeed often finding herself at odds with what we unreflectingly call "disaster assistance," is a recurring theme in the pages to follow.

II

FROM EVACUEES TO EXILES

3

LIFE ON THE ROAD

In the classic tune "When the Levee Breaks," recorded in 1929, Joe McCoy and Memphis Minnie foretell the journey many people in the city would take seventy-six years later to escape Hurricane Katrina's historic floodwaters:[1]

> Mean old levee taught me to weep and moan
> Mean old levee taught me to weep and moan
> Got what it takes to make a Mountain Man leave his home

In 2000, five years before Katrina, Walter Maestri, the emergency manager for Jefferson Parish, made public his assessment that a powerful storm could fill up the bowl that is the Crescent City, topping the roofs of houses and rising as high as three to four stories. In Maestri's scenario the city could be under water for up to ten weeks. While recognizing that getting everyone out of harm's way is more pipe dream than practical policy, Maestri was certain that evacuating the city was the only reasonable option in the event of a calamity of this magnitude.[2] Walter Maestri, as we now know, was all too prophetic in both his warning and his counsel.

On August 28, the day before Katrina made landfall, an alarmed mayor of New Orleans ordered the first mandatory evacuation in the history of the city. With gravitas fitting the moment, Mayor Ray Nagin warned, "This is a threat we've never faced before." His simple command, to get out of town, created for many a mess of complications.[3] For one thing, Katrina's timing could not have been worse for tens of thousands of New Orleans families. The twenty-eighth day of the month is a date on the calendar when the paycheck is spent, or nearly so. The prospect of an emergency trip is likely to stretch if not snap an already thin budget, a problem all too common among Hollygrove's working class.

Hollygrove resident Denise Anders begins her story of evacuating New Orleans with her son a day before the storm:

It's just him and I. Money is tight. What can I bring? So I get the ice chest. We have orange juice, water. . . . We had ham. I made two sandwiches, cut them in half and we had cereal. . . . Let's just pack clothes for five days. . . . Well, we're in Shreveport and I'm crying and panicking. I'm crying out, "Lord, I'm going to have to make sure my savings is right." . . . All night driving. My son was napping in between and the blessing was he would get up. "Mama, wake up!" I was swerving. "Mama get up!"

In her clipped, spur-of-the-moment telling, Denise decants the life of the evacuee in knowing, wrought-iron sentences. Imagine having to move abruptly from the worrisome but more or less predictable life of a single mother to the unmoored life of an evacuee. From the predictable to the wholly unforeseen, she is fleeing ahead of danger on roads leading somewhere, if traffic permits, if money allows, if the car is able. Her only goal is to get on the road, to put distance between her and danger.

The words "emergency" and "evacuation" have a certain affinity for one another. Together they conjure images of unusual events and circumstances, experiences that defy our center of gravity, throwing us off balance if not knocking us down. But there is at least one noteworthy difference in the meaning of these two words. If an emergency is a sudden, unexpected occurrence requiring immediate action, evacuation is the act of protecting oneself and others by withdrawing from a place in an orderly fashion. The definitional emphasis on "orderly" is echoed in the literature on the sociology of disaster. A foundational paper on the topic concludes that

> to the extent that there are research observations, they show that the withdrawal movement itself usually proceeds relatively well. The flight tends to be orderly, reasonable from the perspective of the evacuees, and generally effective in removing people from danger.[4]

Our quarrel with the sentence that flight from danger appears orderly is not that at times it can appear so to others; we suspect it does. Our squabble is with the subject of the sentence. Chances are quite good that "from the perspective of the evacuees," words like "orderly" and "organized" would not capture their immediate and felt experiences of fleeing from harm's reach. Now, had the passage read, "from the perspective of those sociologists who examine evacuation from what Geertz might call an 'experience-distant' vantage point," the abstraction "orderly" might well make sense.[5] But for Denise Anders—who recounts, "All night driving. My son was napping in between and the blessing was he would get up. 'Mama, wake up!' I was swerving. 'Mama get up!'"—fleeing Katrina's wind and water was anything but methodical.

If we move closer to the lived moments of evacuation, if we get inside the car by listening to the accounts of those on the road, the relation of the unforeseen and the flight from danger is plain to see. Denise continues:

> So my sister and her husband, my little niece and her boyfriend, they was at the [New Orleans] convention center. There was a cop that told them he didn't know when the bus was coming. But he had a truck. . . . He was a police officer working but he said he was leaving because he couldn't take it anymore. . . . He said, "I can't take care of y'all but if y'all hide away in the back of my truck, I have to go to Baton Rouge. I'm leaving. I can drop y'all off."

In words that spill out one after another as if they themselves were running from danger, Denise invites us to find some alternative vocabulary for making sense of the lived experiences of evacuation. Far from orderly in the academic or conventional meaning of the word, her sister and her sister's husband and her niece and the niece's boyfriend find themselves on an aleatory journey, a miscellaneous collection of fate-filled moments.

Our task in this chapter is to call to life a few of the interanimating contingencies that make up the moments of evacuation and the experience of being evacuees in Pontchartrain Park and Hollygrove. In doing so we reveal a little of how people cope with a chance-filled world by at least in part not recognizing it for what it is. But there is more afoot in the intersection of evacuation, contingency, and our two neighborhoods. The quantity and quality of the haphazard are not completely random, though they are likely to appear so to those who find themselves on the road. Contingency is typically shaped in part by life chances tethered to the wheel of material well-being. "Material well-being" sounds a bit like an experience-distant abstraction. We can bring it closer to the experiences of the people from the neighborhoods by calling it "cheese."

"CHEESE"

"There's a word heard from time to time in the black community. Some people got it; some people don't. The word is 'cheese,'" explains Cheryl Haden, a college professor who lives in Pontchartrain Park. "Cheese" refers to a variety of things, all of them related to material resources of one sort or another. Cheese might be a credit card, a small square of hard plastic that opens the world of commodities and services to those who own one and keep current with their monthly payments. Or it might be a paycheck for those with jobs, or a dependable car. Cheryl describes the uses of "cheese" in her experience of evacuation:

Okay, where to begin. Well, the difference between me and swimming in floodwater was my American Express card. I'm a middle-class person, I'm a professor at a university. I live within my means; I certainly don't live beyond them. But I don't live anywhere below my means either. I sometimes think of myself as an alligator in the lagoon. I have exactly expanded to the size of the territory that will sustain me.

It was the 29th, which is a day or two before the first payday of the fall semester for me. I'd been living off my summer salary and the little bit of savings that I had. And when we got the notification about the size and the danger of Hurricane Katrina, I used my American Express card and paid for reservations to reserve my room at the Best Western. I happen to have had a car, the car I still have. It was just three years old at the time and in good working order. It had four good tires on it; it didn't overheat. There are so many people who have city cars, just cars that are great for knocking around town and getting where you need to go so that you're not on public transportation or on a bicycle but are not going to survive the drive someplace else. If you don't have a credit card, you can't reserve a hotel room. If you don't have a credit card, you cannot rent a car.

If social class, to borrow from David Harvey, is not some abstract "force that operates outside the web of life, the day-to-day struggles, routines, or the ordinary," its immediacy in human lives will be dramatically enhanced during a flight from impending danger that sends one from home to road.[6] Denise Anders, who lives in Hollygrove, and Cheryl Haden, who lives in Pontchartrain Park, are both homeowners. They are both single moms, each with one child. Both are African American, separated in age by less than ten years. These similarities are striking, but a fundamental difference between them sends these two women on quite different journeys down the evacuation highway. Both women were drawn into a world governed by chance, but they did so with different resources at their disposal. While "chance" has a different look and feel for those with cheese, both stories emphasize the place of fluke in the kismet-filled life on the road.

Cheryl continues:

I wasn't completely hip to the whole contraflow explanation, and I had the book and the map and it didn't make a damn bit of sense to me, so I just tried to leave a day earlier, you know, avoid it entirely. So my sister and I had taken our own cars in the past, but this time, we all rode in my little baby SUV, with my mom and my sister and my daughter and her fish.

Some other people followed us in their cars. Professor Lawrence Jenkins, who's the chair of our department, and Christopher Saucedo, who's a sculpture professor, made up a caravan. A new professor from Canada, Marge, who's since left, also came along, and Andy Arden and his wife, Jen.

We all stayed at the same Best Western on Main Street in Houston because it's . . . about six blocks from the Houston Museum of Fine Arts, really close to the original Ninfa's. Our plan was to have some decent Mexican food and drink martinis. And I was responsible for the tequila, and Marge brought the bourbon, and Christopher had the Irish whiskey. So, we had our plan, we had wives and children and pets, and we were all in the same place at the same time. And we watched the Weather Channel with bated breath.

And we watched this monster grow. We started getting nervous and praying for it to go to Mississippi, and it went to Mississippi, and we were all so relieved. So we all went to Cheesecake Bistro in the Galleria and bought things we shouldn't have and ate too much and drank too much and came back to our hotel and went to sleep. Next morning Lawrence Jenkins was knocking on our hotel room door saying that the city's flooded. And I turned on the television and I saw Wolf Blitzer on CNN, who said that in all likelihood it may be as late as Christmastime, December, before residents were allowed back in their homes.

And I thought, "Oh my God, how are you going deal with this?" So I spoke to my sister about it, and we decided that the first thing we needed to do was get my mom someplace where she would be safe and comfortable while we dealt with her house and my house and my sister's house, because at this point we didn't know.

And I called my cousin Alice because being a black person from New Orleans, people stay here, people live here, people die here, and they're only as limited as their family members who actually move away and are prepared to shelter them from those things that push us out of the city. My cousin Alice's son and wife and daughter had recently bought a home just outside of Atlanta, in Stone Mountain.

Cheryl, her daughter, and her sister left their friends in Houston and made the twelve-hour road trip to Georgia. There they shared a house with dozens of extended family members who were also escaping Katrina's reach.

At one time there were about thirty family members in this one house, and seventeen of them were under the age of ten. No one shut their eyes for ninety-six hours because we had two family members who stubbornly refused to leave New Orleans. And we were watching CNN, and we were hoping to get a glimpse of them but also hoping not to get a glimpse of them. They were both safe, they got put on the bus and put on a plane, and one ended up in Utah, and one ended up in Arizona. Apparently you didn't know where you were going until the plane had taken off.

Okay, we were in Georgia, Stone Mountain, that's where we were. We were in Stone Mountain in Georgia, our New Orleans home is flooded, and all I had was two pair of underwear and one pair of shoes, and you know, two changes of clothes, and that's all my child had. . . . So we're going to Walmart to at least get something. I didn't know how much money I really had anymore. Whitney Banks were sort of shut down. I lived on my American Express card. They were excellent; I will always be an American Express card customer. They said, "We're so sorry this happened to you, buy whatever you want to, you don't have a credit limit." They didn't charge us interest for six months. They asked if we needed doctors, if we needed to buy a car.

One of my former students who I lived with during the renovation of the house, Bonnie Slaughter, and her husband, Scott, she called and she asked me, "Do you have a car? I'm going send you $5,000." And I said, "Well, I actually don't need any money right now." A guy I dated, I can't even remember, called to see if we were okay or if we needed anything, and he had two cars and he wanted to send one to us. And I said, "We have a car," but you know, these are just some of the people who popped up in my life. . . .

So, you know, I got a job at Walmart because I didn't know if my university would still be in business when I returned.

Cheryl recounts a story that begins with what she anticipated would be a short, pleasant trip out of town, an unscheduled vacation to avoid a hurricane that would most likely miss the city, as most do. Some people in New Orleans call these unexpected trips an "e-vacation," a play on "evacuation." In the initial hours of her evacuation, Cheryl, accompanied by family and friends, acted on the basis of a well-thought-out plan to move a caravan of kin and colleagues to a comfortable location in Houston, one well-suited for those who enjoy the arts, an array of spirits, and good food. From there they would wait it out in reasonable comfort the passage of the hurricane.

Calamity, however, in all its guises, from the random accident to breached seawalls weakened by years of neglect, hangs suspended over our best-laid plans, ready to change the course of our lives in the most abrupt and unexpected manner. Freud would have us "treat chance as worthy of determining our fate" in our most quotidian of moments.[7] Life in disaster leaves us no choice in the matter.

Once it was clear that Hurricane Katrina had no intention of avoiding an opportunity to demonstrate New Orleans' poorly built and maintained levee system, her capricious winds shoved the errant waters of the lakes and canals into the city, turning Cheryl's planned evacuation into a protean, shape-shifting journey, a trek that takes her from a spontaneous holiday in Houston to Stone Mountain, Georgia, life lived among thirty-plus relatives, and finally to a job at a local Walmart. While on the road Cheryl encounters a former student who offers to send her $5,000. She hears from the people at American Express that her credit is limitless and no interest charges will accrue to her balance for six months. People from her past pop up to offer her material assistance.

It takes no great leap of the imagination to connect Cheryl's relative good fortune in this turn of events to her social and material resources. Cheese, we might say, has far more than an accidental connection to daily life. But all is not shaped or predicted by material resources. For a middle-class, single mom on the road fleeing a hurricane, cheese intersects with the mutable force of the accidental.

There is little that is predictable about her evacuation experience; it is more a cascade of colliding coincidences than a prudent, well-conceived journey contrived from a first-this-then-that plan of action. If we stop at this juncture and conjure up an orderly abstraction of this personal account of bedlam bordering on entropy, we risk losing what is most forceful about Cheryl's story: to wit, its blow-on-blow account of fate and fortuity. It is plain, however, that the fragments of credit, money, friends, and family from which she cobbled together her journey are not themselves wholly coincidental; they are, rather, connected in some fashion to the supple, elastic materials of class that reach deep into the tissue of human life lived in both its banal and its unnerving moments.

Consider now Denise Anders's account, beginning with her decision to get out of town. Denise left the city in haste, her son in tow, with a few sandwiches, some cereal, and a little money; she drove madly out of harm's way. No e-vacation for her. By the time she left, it was all too clear that much of New Orleans was destined to be under water:

> Well, Saturday morning, watching the news, it was just in my spirit. I was
> scared. It was like, we need to leave. So me being a single parent, I'm like,
> who can I get to leave with me because gas and a hotel room can be ex-

pensive. So I called up friends and family members. "The storm is coming our way. We need to go." They like, "We're doing this, we're staying, we have a party." . . . So I'm panicking. I'm at the gas station getting gas. I call a girlfriend of mine; she says her sister has some rooms in Tyler. I said, "I can't get anybody from my family to go. I may just stay." And she said, "No, you can come with us." I had never heard of Tyler, Texas, let alone been to Tyler, Texas.

We get to Tyler. It took us sixteen hours. We get to Tyler at six in the morning. We drove all night. My girlfriend, her husband, and kids, drove in one car. Us in another. They didn't have a cell phone, so it's not like I can call them. I'm just trying to keep up with them 'cause I didn't know where I was going. So when we get to Tyler the next morning we go get breakfast. We . . . see what's happening to New Orleans.

Denise evacuated with her son, but like Cheryl and so many people in New Orleans, her kin, people she carries in her heart and mind, would fast become a part of her life on the road:

I could not get in contact with my family in New Orleans for a couple of days. The plan was my sister who worked at Days Inn on Read Boulevard would take everybody with her. So everybody went to the Days Inn, and the last I heard from them the hotel was flooding and they had to go onto the roof. There were police officers and their families on the roof too. Boats came to get them. They said the boats would come back for everyone else. But they didn't. The police got saved but not my family.

I spoke with someone at the shelter that was doing rescue, and I told them about my family. So a boat finally came. It got my mom, two of my sisters, two of my brother-in-laws, and my little niece and her boyfriend. But then the boat capsized twice. They said my mom almost drowned flipping over. Then they had to go to the convention center. They were at the convention center for, like, three days.

Finally my mom and all get picked up by a helicopter. They fly them to Louis Armstrong Airport. They took a jet from Louis Armstrong to Arlington, Texas. So I had to drive from Tyler to Arlington, Texas, to pick them up. So a guy at the hotel who knew one of my friends said, "I know how to get to Arlington, I'll ride with you." So on the way to Arlington my truck started smoking. I never had a problem with my truck before. So, we can't drive past seventy or it starts smoking, something with the fuel pump, I don't know.

So it takes us like five hours to get to Arlington. And there are all these people at the airport, we go from check-out place to check-out place trying to find them. So we finally get them and we drive back to Tyler. We were able to get another room at the hotel. It was like five in my room and five in another room. So we get together, then we get the money split up.

Meanwhile, Denise's niece and her two children, who had somehow ended up in Houston, were told they had to leave the shelter that was housing them. She told her niece to come to Tyler, where she would be near her family and could get care for her asthmatic son:

I told her they'll give you the nebulizer; they'll give you medicine. So my niece came to Tyler. That was a relief because she was crying every day. So I took her to the shelter. She got the nebulizer and all the medicines. So it was her and I together. She said, "Well, at least I have you."

Denise was able to pay for a third hotel room to house her niece and her niece's children. At last, though far from New Orleans, more than a dozen members of the Anders clan were together. The night her niece arrived, some local folks they had met in Tyler chipped in some cash that Denise distributed among family members.

But even with the help of strangers, money was running low. The motel was only a stop along the way. Denise found a new apartment complex nearby that let people move in without a deposit and offered one month's free rent. Several family members moved into the new apartments, while she moved to a nearby duplex and took her son and mother along with her. Good fortune struck again in the form of a $500 gift card and donations of "blankets, comforters, china, utensils, toilet tissue, everything" from a local church.

In her animated voice, Denise continues:

When everybody had a cot or bed, a place to stay, we started a routine. Every morning we got up, we piled up as many as we could into the truck, dropped them at the shelter, come back, filled up again and back to the shelter. The shelter fed us. So it took two or three trips to get everybody at the shelter, then to bring everybody back.

On that first week of driving back and forth, on my last trip of the day, it was me, my son, my sister, and my brother-in-law in the truck. I'm in the middle lane and there's an F-150 and a Yukon on the side of me. Coming in the opposite direction, this lady runs a red light. She hit the truck and the SUV and smashed us in the middle. I was okay initially. My brother-in-law, he was in the back, he was hurt. Maybe a week later, my back begins to hurt. I started getting pain from my neck all the way down. So maybe for three weeks I was going to therapy.

Fleeing harm's way, Denise ran headlong into a haphazard world with its own troubles. Her place in that world was complicated by the trials and tribulations of at least fifteen other displaced family members all short on money. There is little in Denise's story that foreshadows what might happen next.

CHEESE AND KIN

The importance of family is woven into the evacuation stories we collected in Hollygrove and Pontchartrain Park. Not surprisingly, many of these stories sort themselves out by the relative access to cheese. Contingency and its sometimes obvious, sometimes nuanced connection to class is underlined in the following two stories about evacuation and kin. In Gwen Rigby's almost effortless effort to reach her kin and Jesse's angst-filled search for his brother, we meet once again at the intersection of material well-being and life in disaster.

Gwen Rigby from Hollygrove works for Amtrak. A practical person, Miss Rigby planned her evacuation around access to train routes that would take her to friends scattered about the country. Gwen knew that several relatives were stranded on the causeway bridge and at the convention center in the first few days after the storm. She desperately needed to know her kin were okay. A text message would do:

> Once I texted everybody and found out that everybody was okay, it was alright. But then I couldn't find my grandmother. Come to find out my grandmother was evacuated to Houston. So I stayed there long enough to get her situated, and I went on. When I was hopping from train to train at that particular time, I was thinking about my family. "Where are they? Are they okay?" Because even though I could text them, it was a long time before they texted me back. I really didn't get in contact with them until I was in Chicago, which is the reason why I nixed my plans to go from Chicago to Atlanta and to go from Chicago to Houston. So that's all I was thinking about. I wasn't thinking about the house, what it looked like. I was just wondering where was everyone?

Jesse Gray, who calls Hollygrove home, might be speaking for most people in both neighborhoods when he notes with a raw plainness, "Oh, yes, it's important to know where your family is when you're in a disaster. Because you worry if you don't know where your people are." Jesse evacuated and lost touch with his brother Bo, who rode out the storm in his home just a couple blocks from Jesse's house:

We lost contact with Bo. We didn't know where he was. It was about three weeks before we heard. We thought he had drowned. We made contact with one of my first cousins, and he says Bo was in a boat rescuing people throughout the neighborhood. You know, but we still, we hadn't heard nothing from Bo, and we lost contact with my first cousin 'cause he was still in New Orleans too. Then Bo called, finally, and I remember crying because I thought he was dead. I remember crying on the phone, I was so glad to hear his voice.

WHITHER THE CHEESE

While we've no scale or measure affirming this, these varied accounts of evacuation allow us to discern the subtle connections between the agile reach of cheese into the moment-by-moment events, circumstances, and coincidences of evacuation. It might be said we learn far more about the reach of market forces into the interstices of ordinary human life when all hell breaks loose than we do in the quotidian world of the mundane.

As with Cheryl, Denise, and countless other evacuees with their varying resources—or well-practiced resourcefulness—so too for Gwen and Jesse: the trouble to locate kin along the road appeared in one case to be relatively easy while in another to be a source of prolonged worry and concern. In their cases, "cheese" explains a good deal of the variance.

No one would relish being forced to flee home in the face of impending disaster. But a close-up look at the life of an evacuee suggests that once on the road, the relative access to material resources plays a part in sorting out who is likely to move about in space and time with a measure of confidence and who will find the unforeseen just around every turn. If uncertainty is a moment when it is impossible to contrive a reliable probability distribution for outcomes, those whom disasters push to the road are likely to face more or less of it based, at least in part, on their relative access to cheese.

For many if not most residents of Pontchartrain Park and Hollygrove, the long, strange trip of evacuation would prove to be only the beginning. With nowhere to live in a city brought to its knees by turbid waters freed from the shoddy levees meant to contain them, returning to the city would set them on often meandering journeys from evacuee to exile before finding a way home.

4

FROM THE ROAD TO EXILE

You shall leave everything loved most dearly, and this is the
shaft of which the bow of exile shoots first. You shall prove how
salt is the taste of another man's bread and how hard is the
way up and down another man's stairs.

DANTE ALIGHIERI, "PARADISE"

The life of an evacuee, like that of all sentient persons, is not without some navigable logic. But what makes this life unique is its characteristic drift. Denise and Cheryl are carried along from experience to experience, from space to space, by currents and forces that didn't override the rudder of the self but did make steerage a continuous challenge. Life on the road is lived in the shadow of contingency, though just how the unforeseen is likely to occur and how we respond to it is linked in numerous ways to the complexities of material circumstances, as we have seen.[1]

But the mutable life of the evacuee does hold out one promise with some surety: returning home will occur in the not-too-distant future. No matter how buffeted by the winds of chance, most evacuees fleeing most hurricanes know that their time on the road is not without a predictable endpoint.[2] The storm warning will be canceled or the evacuation order rescinded, and return home in one, two, or three days is likely if not certain. Hurricane Katrina, however, was not like most hurricanes.

Carolyn Chimes is a real estate agent and resident of Hollygrove. She expresses what most evacuees in both neighborhoods were likely feeling and thinking:

> Well, I was thinking initially we would be gone about two days at the most. We didn't have hardly any clothes; we didn't bring hardly anything. And I said, "Well, we'll be back, you know, two days we should be back," so that's how everybody packed. We didn't have the space to put a bunch

of suitcases. So we didn't even think that way. We thought basically, this is an overnight, two days at the most, and then we come back. Who could imagine leaving knowing their house would be destroyed? That's too much to think about. I couldn't even think like that.

When the water stopped its advance into the city, 80 percent of New Orleans lay like a half-exposed Atlantis for more than two weeks. Stewing in a fusty, toxic soup for this protracted time were tens of thousands of houses and apartments. Immediate return for most of the city's residents was impossible. Tens of thousands of evacuees were about to become exiles, expelled from their houses and apartments for indefinite periods by a historic flood in a seeming alliance with what would soon prove to be inept local, state, and federal responses.

A successful accountant and financial consultant, Michael Carrington grew up in Pontchartrain Park and purchased a house just across the street from his homestead. Like most who found themselves on the road fleeing the storm, Michael had a measure of confidence that he would be returning in just a day or two. He was mistaken:

> Well, when I was in Shreveport and we were all glued to the TV for days watching everything unfold with the hurricane being a near miss and we dodged a bullet to now there are reports of a levee break, multiple levee breaks, now the water is pouring into the city and no one can stop it, thinking to myself, "Did it get to my neighborhood?" . . . When I first saw a picture of my neighborhood, I could see there was water in the neighborhood, but I couldn't tell how deep it was looking at it straight above. What was I looking at? I wasn't sure. I really felt myself anxious to know how deep was the water. . . . Just how deep was it?

Michael would not move back to New Orleans for a year and a half. He spent the first three weeks of his evacuation sleeping in the study of a friend's spacious suburban house in Bossier City, Louisiana. He reunited with his parents at the home of another friend in Brusly, Louisiana, before renting an apartment in nearby Baton Rouge. He finally returned to Pontchartrain Park in March 2007 when he moved into his parents' freshly renovated home.

Jesse, a retired cement finisher and lifelong resident of Hollygrove, could not anticipate just how long a time his life would be changed by Hurricane Katrina. But his story of turning from an evacuee into an exile differs from Michael's, reflecting the not-so-subtle ways the abstractions of class shape the immediate course of life:

We left. We evacuated to Amite, Louisiana, . . . my mother's sister and them are up there, and when we got up there, they had twenty-seven of us in one house, twenty-seven in the house. That's right, so you can imagine trying to use the one bathroom or something like that . . . We usually go there every year when there's a storm or something coming, we go up there and after it pass over we'll come right back home . . . But not this time. This time we stayed up there two years! . . . You know how it is when you staying in your kinfolks' house, let me tell you.

Over time, many of Jesse's twenty-six family members would find other housing. Jesse needed to stay with his mother's sister in part because his mother needed the assistance her sister could provide, and it was far cheaper than trying to rent an apartment or house. But Jesse's words about staying with kin hint at the difficulties that may follow life lived for protracted periods contingent on the compassion of others. Compassion, we will soon see, often can more easily be mustered and sustained when those providing it have themselves sufficient resources to accommodate the needs of others.

Though differences in material circumstances helped shape Michael's experiences of evacuation one way and Jesse's another, they and many of those who lived in Pontchartrain Park and Hollygrove were thrown into a world Homer would have understood. In this move from evacuee to exile, each person became his or her own Odysseus struggling at times against all apparent odds to outwit fate and return home. And like Odysseus, who was tormented by the gods of fate as he sought a way home, Michael and Jesse journeyed home in anything but tranquil waters.[3]

SPACE IS TO EVACUATION AS PLACE IS TO EXILE

In this chapter we examine the transition from the lived experience of evacuation to life in exile and the prolonged struggle to return home. Da Vinci found ordinary life "full of countless causes that never enter" our awareness.[4] Life in evacuation and exile begs us to multiply those "countless causes" by ten and add a few more. But the experiences of evacuation and exile, though tethered to the unforeseen, do differ one from the other. The dozens of stories we collected about life in this stretch of time away from the haven of home drew our attention to the distinction between space and place. One might consider the distinction in the form of an "if then" statement: If evacuation is lived in space, then exile is lived in search of place.[5]

The life of an evacuee is lived on the road with temporary respites in hotels, the houses of friends and relatives, schools, churches, convention centers, and other shelters set aside for those fleeing harm's reach. Evacuees' beds, cots, sofas, and floors are provisional, they reason, short-term arrangements until the official call to return home.

It is the road away from home and the road that leads home as danger wanes that orient the evacuees in space and time. The lived experience of evacuation itself, the time on the road, is told in one way by the residents of Hollygrove and Pontchartrain Park; the far longer time spent living elsewhere is a telling of a different sort. If the experience of evacuation summons the hard-edged bluntness of Denise Anders's words and phrasing, perhaps it is because, in part, roads are more likely to be experienced as widths, distances, directions, and angles, physical vectors intentionally created to move us along from one place to another. Describing life on the road invites a spare, bony account.

LIFE IN PLACE

If a road is more a space, a place is a cartography of meaning, a site somewhere in the universe upon which we stand and make some reasonable sense of ourselves, others, and the world about us. We might imagine the extended duration of life in exile as something akin to Burroughs's "interzone," a sort of fixed and unchanging somewhere else, a life lived betwixt and between.[6] While there is a certain charm to this analogy, it ignores our human need to be someplace.

Place envelopes us. A mosaic of the physical, social, cultural, and psychological, it is from inside the security of place that we can fend off life's challenges and respond to our own needs and those of others. At once familiar, inviting our attachment and helping to secure our identity, place in exile, simply put, makes life sufferable.[7]

When the waters flooded the city, one thing was certain: the most familiar place of all, the house, was no longer habitable. Common to life in Hollygrove and Pontchartrain Park was an almost preternatural connection to houses. Most middle-class and a growing number of working-class Americans are peripatetic, moving on average every six or seven years.[8] The people and families making up the populations of Hollygrove and Pontchartrain Park, however, are not. They "stay put," as the expression goes, in their homes, often for decades. In 2000, 54 percent of Hollygrove residents and 78 percent of residents in Pontchartrain Park had lived in their houses for a minimum of eleven years.[9] Cheryl Haden understands:

I think that the black community, at least the older black community, has a different philosophy about real estate than younger black people or people of other races. The house you buy is the house you live in; it's the house you die in. I don't think the majority of black people in New Orleans who are my age or older think in terms of the starter house. When I look at this house, I think, "Fine, when I get too old to go upstairs, the good news is, there's no upstairs." That works. It's the house I plan to live in when I retire.

Many if not most residents trace their lineage deep into the histories of their two neighborhoods. Houses were the physical places that connected generations of family members. Aging parents were more likely to pass their houses on to their children or grandchildren than to put them up for sale. It is in these intergenerational ties that exile for residents of these urban neighborhoods is freighted with more than the cultural and psychological weight of the bond between house and self. Complicating place as a physical location is the almost primordial need to know the whereabouts of immediate and extended kin. Absent this knowledge, fashioning a place from one's immediate material circumstances would, for many, prove to be impossible.

In short, memories, those singular ones connecting the present with the past, creating some sense of personal continuity across time, and the collective ones linking immediate and extended kin in a reticulate web of relationship are entwined with the joists, sills, and soffits of the homestead. For the residents of Pontchartrain Park and Hollygrove who evacuated New Orleans only to watch from afar as their city filled with water, the struggle to find place in exile was about to begin. For not a few residents, Dante's warning to the exiled—"hard is the way up and down another man's stairs"— captures the work required of each of them to maintain some sense of personal dignity and sanity as a person in need of the goodwill of others. And herein lies the rub.

THE SCARLET LETTER "E"

Like the scarlet letter "A" that Hawthorne placed on Hester Prynne's breast, many exiles might well have wondered if an "E" was visible to those who knew they were among the tens of thousands displaced by the floodwaters.[10] Marva Wright, legendary New Orleans' blues singer, gives a soulful voice to their concern in a verse from Benny Turner's "Katrina Blues":

People are nice. They say,
"Welcome to our home."
But they start acting funny
when we stayed too long.[11]

Jesse recalls the trouble he found when people "acted funny" during a long stay in his aunt's house following the flooding of the city:

And . . . when you were driving up there, the idea in your mind, right, was that you were gonna turn around the next day or the day after, drive back down here. Well, . . . we saw it on the news where the flood was rising in New Orleans. We knew we couldn't return to our neighborhood. We just didn't know for how long.

We was staying with my mother's sister. We stayed in her house. It was me, my wife, and my mom. . . . Ah, you know, staying in other people's houses. You know it was rough, man, real rough. I had others to look after. I had my mother to look after, plus two nieces. I had to take care of my mama, she's eighty-eight years old, you know. She suffers with congestive heart failure. She was in and out the hospital, so I didn't know which way to turn . . .

And I paid the water bill, the light bill, the gas bill; I paid them all. I wanted to pay our keep. And it was rough, rough, being in other people's house for so long. Her son, my aunt's son, my cousin, he was there seems like every day. He'd pull up in the driveway and yell, "Who is that?" gruffly, "What they want?" I like to had a nervous breakdown when he did that.

Jesse's "E" begins to burn crimson in what seemed at first to be the welcoming quarters of his mother's sister's house. Acutely self-conscious of staying too long under his aunt's roof, caring for his sick mother and young nieces, in dread of his cousin's taunting question "Who is that?"—Jesse lived a step or two away from collapse.

Clara Carrington, retired from the University of New Orleans and a resident of Pontchartrain Park, tells a story about how the good intentions of others can unintentionally create a feeling of unease, pushing an exile out of one place and into another:

They took all of us in, and those people treated us so good. Like I tell people all the time, the last day those people treated us as well as they did the first day when we came. They were really nice to us. We were fortunate. These people had a house about the same size as our house, and they were able to give us a place to stay. . . . It was seven people, a baby, and a dog.

I tell you I got to the place, though, where these people, it was really nice being at their house, but . . . this is what they did: they turned on every television in their house—and they have a lot of televisions, and they kept them on the station that was showing the flooding day in and day out. So I got to a place where I didn't want to see it anymore. . . . I think I just got down, depressed, and disgusted with seeing the situation after a month or a month and a half. . . . I was talking to my sisters in Cleveland. I told them about the television and this constant stuff going on. . . . My sisters got together and sent me a ticket north to Cleveland.

Sometimes the "E" burned in public, in the civic spaces of day-to-day life. "And they were wonderful people in Baton Rouge," Cheryl recalls:

Everyone could not have been nicer. But there was one evil bitch at the Walmart who was furious because she said all of the people from New Orleans were taking up the parking spaces and drinking all of the Diet Coke. And I said, "Well, I can't speak for anyone else, but I came here with someone else, we carpooled, and I'm drinking single-barrel Jack Daniels only. I have not touched the Diet Coke since I arrived."

Cheryl knew she was someone who fled from danger and was now in a certain sense a person out of place. While she was quite familiar with Baton Rouge, eighty miles northwest of New Orleans, she was there at that moment not as a professor or a casual visitor but as a displaced person, an exile of sorts. Likewise, Jesse knew his aunt and his cousins. He'd visited their house many times but never in exile. The acid tone of the question posed daily by his cousin—"What they want?"—never let him forget he was there at the mercy of others, more a ward of the house than a guest. Clara's "E" was less feverish, rather lukewarm; it was not insulting, nor did it strike at her sense of self-worth. It simply made the televisions scattered about her newfound place insufferable reminders of a catastrophe she would like the opportunity to forget, if only momentarily.

Hester Prynne learns over time to embrace her scarlet letter, turning it from a symbol of shame to one of pride. But Hester, unlike Jesse, Clara, Cheryl, and so many others, was not at the mercy of friends, relatives, and strangers. In Hawthorne's tale, she had a modest house and a sufficient income, and she was not forced to fashion places from spaces while escaping arguably the worst urban disaster in American history. Katrina threw hundreds of thousands of people into exile, each one needing to settle his or her account with a life lived in and out of place. How does one redeem the absence of home?

When the waters flooded the city, one thing was certain: no one was in control of how things were going. For those thousands of people on the road and for those left in the city, there was no reliable source offering concrete information and resources to help them make some reasonable sense of what had happened to them and what the future held. What choices are there? How do I choose? How certain am I that this choice will bring the anticipated results? Michael Carrington could be speaking for those who lived in Pontchartrain Park and Hollygrove when he says simply, "We knew our lives were changing. We just didn't know how much and for how long at the time." And those in nominal charge of the disaster were just as unaware as Michael of how much and for how long. What if the knowledge we cannot know is essential to us?

There were no coordinated local, state, or federal plans to move exiles from their makeshift places back to their homes. The great diaspora that almost emptied the city of its human inhabitants was met with a mishmash of disparate public- and private-sector resources thrown together with no systematic map for identifying or accessing them.[12] Finding resources and making choices during this period was a personal matter.

The life of each exile quickly became a cobbled-together solution to a confluence of ecological and organizational contradictions. In the end it was a convergence of human determination, call it agency, and the ambulant, peripatetic chances, opportunities, and frustrations that presented themselves in no necessarily orderly manner that together became the search for a place in exile and eventually a road home.

Jo Johnston, a resident of Pontchartrain Park, is describing the injury that forced her to retire early from a teaching position in the New Orleans school system and secure a Social Security pension: "I broke my right ankle . . . in 2003. . . . So, I have two plates, nuts, bolts, screws, and two rods and three holes in my right leg." Jo lived in the Park for more than a half century and saw her house as a legacy and a tribute to her parents' tenacity:

> This is a family home that I live in. It was bought by my parents after World War II. Pontchartrain Park was developed for Afro-Americans after World War II. Most of the property was bought either on the G.I. Bill or some kind of commercial loan. My parents fought for the property. They were hard workers.

A robust woman in spite of her disability, she was fifty-three when Katrina came ashore and headed toward the Crescent City.

I guess that Thursday before it hit, the news media was talking about evacuating the city and we needed to get out. We weren't afraid because we had hurricanes in the past and we thought, "Three or four days and we'll be back." So, nobody was worried or anything. We thought it would just be like it was before. You leave for a little while, come back, clean up, start over. But this time, with Miss Katrina, it wasn't the case. We rode. It was one-two-three-four-six of us in a little compact sedan. No room to move with our luggage and stuff that we had. We left here about 4, 4:30 that morning, and we arrived in Houston Saturday morning. We stayed in hotels for about maybe two weeks until the money ran out. Then we went to the Houston Convention Center. We lived in the convention center from September to November.

Jo and her friend Julie were asked to leave the Houston Convention Center to make room for the unending stream of families with children and people needing special medical attention.

"I MOVED A TOTAL OF FIFTEEN TIMES IN A YEAR AND A HALF . . . I'M TIRED OF MOVING"

Well, they didn't have room for us anymore at the center. They said they had ran out of resources to accommodate everybody. So we said okay. Well, it was just two of us, myself and my friend . . . and you had people with kids and everything, so we stood out on the street corner at the back of the convention center by the Hilton hotel, 'cause we didn't have anywhere to go. . . . A minister stopped and he asked if we were alright, and we told him yes, we were.

And at that moment then we discovered that we were reading the same part of the Bible. We didn't know it, my girlfriend was on one side of a bench and I was on the other side of a bench and we were both reading Amos, the book of Amos. And the book of Amos told everything that happened in New Orleans. So we were fine, we knew God was in the mix of it, so we didn't worry, we just didn't have anywhere to stay.

After a long while a lady came and picked us up off the street corner with all our belongings. And she said, "Well, I know somebody that knows somebody that knows a friend that knows somebody." I can't think of the lady's name offhand, I'm sorry. And we went to her house for awhile and we stayed and she took in one-two-three, about three other families. And her family moved downstairs.

We couldn't stay there forever . . . pretty soon we were back on the corner. There we met this young man from Yellow Cab. His name was Dave.

We told him what had happened; he brought us to the First Street United Methodist Church. They gave us canned goods and a couple other things that we could eat. When that ran out we started eating little bitty candy suckers. We was eating anything, it really didn't matter.

At some point they came and told us they have this woman's shelter. New Hope, no, Star Hope, a children and woman's shelter. So, they brought us there, dropped us off, we registered. And we slept on the floor for the first night that we were there. And we got us hot meals, and we were able to take a bath, and . . . do some other things. But, we couldn't stay.

They were overcrowded at the time. They had put in as much people as they could. And I think they had a fire marshal law or whatever that said they were overcrowded. So the only place we knew to go was back on that street corner, 'cause we knew how to get there. So we went back to the bench.

I moved a total of fifteen times in a year and a half, between the time of Katrina and getting back home to New Orleans. And I'm tired of moving.

Our ordinary lives are arranged geographically and temporally. Each of us in the moment, in real time, exists in a here, a place from which we can make sense of the material world about us.[13] This "here," a living room, garage, place of work, or perhaps just a bench, is a place from which I can orient and connect myself to the visual and the auditory, to the common stock of perceptions and meanings that together make up my immediate world. From this "here" the world takes on a certain self-evidence, a kind of "and so forth and so on" predictability. Moreover, as we move from one here to another we know with reasonable certainty that we can return to a previous here and always do again what we typically do in that place.[14] These two commonsense assumptions, "and so forth and so on" and "I can always do it again," help to create and sustain the security of place, a knowable world, one we can navigate with some measure of confidence.

It is by way of these ideas that we can glimpse how Jo and Julie begin the life of the exile, a world with its own particular collage of "heres." This short passage identifies a "here," a geographic spot on the streets of Houston: "So, the only place we knew to go was back on that street corner, because we knew how to get there. So we went back." From the bench on this corner, they reasoned, they "could always do it again." The "it" in this instance was finding their way from the corner to some dwelling with beds and, ideally, utilities. Jo continues:

The Star of Hope picked us up again from the corner and gave us the information for a community center that helped us get an apartment. And it was pretty nice. The neighbors in the community was very nice. I had a major bus line about a block away from where I was, I had a Super Walmart, a neighborhood Walmart, I had a post office, the small corner store, so I was fine, sort of. FEMA helped us with the rent at first but stopped paying for utilities.

We lived without utilities for months. My solution to that was—get home before it gets dark. It was cold; it was the wintertime. That meant no electricity, no refrigerator, nowhere to cook food, no nothing, so I would go to the store and buy cold cuts. And the windowsill—I had put up a window shade and blinds. Well, in between the window shade and the blind I was using the ledge on the windowsill as my refrigeration. So, I would have maybe cold cuts on there and a thing of juice, and that's how we lived for several months.

In her description of adapting to life without utilities by fashioning her own version of refrigeration, Jo reminds us of a theme that threads its way throughout our story: To recover from disaster is to fashion a world from the change and ruin about us that is self-evident—if not without its troubles—at least until further notice. What is the root human task in the wake of disaster other than fashioning anew a familiar place, a here that is good enough to support a modicum of the human need for familiarity and repetition?[15]

But catastrophes are times when place might well become less than estimable, elude the calculable, and push a person into an environment that is quite simply not good enough to support the ongoing demands of self and body.

THE PLACELESSNESS OF PLACE

Aubrey Gilman was fifty-two years old when the storm surge pushed the water up and over the Seventeenth Street Canal, flooding his house and those of so many others in Hollygrove. He evacuated with his wife to her brother's house in rural Mississippi. Aubrey could not afford to be unemployed. When his employer called him back to work, he was there the next day, on time. The demands of his job in tandem with a palpable anxiety about his house in Hollygrove colluded to push Aubrey to a space betwixt and between two places; neither one alone nor both together were sufficient to make of him *persona en locata*, a person in place. Rather, Aubrey's story sheds light on what a geographer once called "the placelessness of place."[16]

"UNFORTUNATELY, I STRETCHED MYSELF OUT AND HAD A HEART ATTACK"

We thought we were going to come right back the next day. But it wasn't so. The water was here, and fortunately we made it up to Mississippi. . . . We stayed up there with my brother-in-law. My job is at Boh Brothers. I am a laborer. They told me to come back to New Orleans to work on that Highway 11 bridge here. Right after the storm, we had to jump on it. That bridge that flipped over . . . It was kind of hard for me to come back and forth to the city . . . and the problem was me driving 100 miles every day back and forth to come to work. . . .

It was seven of us in a little house in Mississippi. That was hard, you know, back and forth. My thing was I leave in the morning in the dark and get back home in the dark. I leave at three in the morning to get here for seven or six and knock off sometimes eight or nine at night to drive back, get a couple hours' sleep, drive right back to work.

When I drove back to town, I don't know if it was the smell of dead bodies, but the air was rotten. You had to have a shot to come here and work, a tetanus shot on account of the dead bodies and the flies. The flies were humongous, those big old green flies. It was a mess. Smelly water and flies and the National Guard every now and then would drop a little case of water to us working on the Highway 11 bridge.

Four months I did that and it took a toll on me. I couldn't work for Boh Brothers on weekends because I was trying to get my house together. As it was, I worked twelve hours a day, five days a week. They wanted me to work seven days a week, twelve hours. I needed the money, but I couldn't do that. I had to work on my house and get my stuff together.

Mr. Gilman would work during the week for Boh Brothers and return on the weekends to work on his flooded house in Hollygrove. He recalls first walking into his water-ravaged house:

I was hoping I didn't cross no snakes. I came through the door. . . . Clothes was everywhere, icebox was against the door there; the stove was float-ing around in the house. No time to rest. I said, "Well, I'm going to come here and tear it down today and start over tomorrow." On the weekends I'm working in the house. Sometime I'd come to my house, I'd be so exhausted. I walk in and turn around, get back in the truck and go. I'd leave. I'd drive back to Mississippi. I'd drive right there and get to the door, I'd be so tired. . . . My wife said, "When you going to rest?" . . . I tell her I'm just trying to get back to where we can have a normal life.

My mind was just [on] getting my family back in this house because we were staying in somebody else's house, and it's kind of rough sleeping on an air mattress and laying on the floor. Unfortunately, I stretched myself out and had a heart attack. I had two stents put in my chest.

Aubrey Gilman narrates in plain prose the consequences of living in exile unable to restore a place from which life would be, at the very least, tolerable. For several months Aubrey slept a little each night in a house not his own. He worked on a bridge a hundred miles from that house in his hometown, a city that no longer looked, smelled, or behaved in a manner that invited him to return. Finally, Aubrey crossed the threshold of his house to find it was no longer home but a surreal kind of chaos.

But if we pay specific attention to how Mr. Gilman experienced his city and his house, we can imagine ways in which place, the once familiar and comfortable, becomes placeless. Aubrey's story illustrates how we can move from emplaced to displaced without going anywhere. Disaster can move us from inside to outside the commonplace by transforming what is common about that place into something anomalous, like a floating stove, or dangerous, like rotting bodies and bacteria-carrying flies.

The stories Jo and Aubrey tell of life in exile are poignant reminders of the significance of place in our lives. They also hint at the ways in which subtle differences in material circumstances play themselves out in the lived experience of disaster. Jo and Aubrey are demographically akin. If we take a broad brush, we would paint them both as middle class. But if we begin to sort out the details, what we find is that Aubrey is a "laborer," Jo a retired teacher on disability and pension benefits. Neither is well off, but one has a steady, uninterrupted income stream, while the other still must work to get paid. In these two stories we glimpse once again the subtle, nuanced way differences in material well-being traverse the mundane and catastrophic moments in our lives.

CONCLUSION

Hurricane Katrina reminds us that we are wise to be at the ready to revise our standard nomenclature and models of people and catastrophe. While the study of evacuation has been a prominent if somewhat myopic topic in the sociology of disaster, there are few if any studies on exile.[17] As the severity of disaster increases and threatens ever greater swaths of the human landscape, it is reasonable to assume that a greater number of people will be forced to flee their homes only to discover they are unable to return for long stretches of time. Sartre anticipated the exiled worlds into which Jesse, Michael, Cheryl, Clara, Aubrey, and Jo were thrown. He called them "metastable," fragile arrangements, easily broken and in need of constant patching up.[18] These worlds would come to an end at different times and for different reasons for the people we interviewed.

Evacuation and exile, however, are only two among other trials facing the residents of Hollygrove and Pontchartrain Park. There were at least two more noteworthy ordeals that would mark their rites of passage to that coveted identity, "disaster survivor." The first required them to navigate the minefield of disaster assistance; the second demanded that they rebuild their houses amidst the muddle and mess of a broken city. It is these two tests of human character we take up in Part III.

Returning home, however, would be determined by more than the great flood. For many living in exile, negotiating with family members over who, when, how, and sometimes where return would take place required some kind of consensus before the journey home began. Moreover, most would need to attend almost daily to the fuzzy requirements of shape-shifting state and federal relief programs that seemed to require new documents or signatures at every turn. And as if navigating this complex world from afar was not enough, those exiles lucky enough to have homeowners' insurance and the far fewer with flood insurance kept cell phone vigils waiting for often overworked and inexperienced adjusters to return calls about what were, in many cases, contested settlement offers.[19]

And all of this waiting, negotiating with family, struggling against opaque government relief programs, and fighting for some semblance of fairness with insurance companies would take place in hotel rooms, gymnasiums, convention centers, the occasional apartments, and the homes of friends or extended kin. Life was lived in spaces not their own, more often than not among people who agreed—until further notice—to assist them. And these spaces were nested in civic spheres, neighborhoods, towns, and cities that perhaps were somewhat familiar but just as likely new and unknown. If contingency had a face, it would look much like life in exile.

III

TRAVERSING AND REBUILDING

IT'S AVAILABLE, BUT IS IT ACCESSIBLE?
TRAVERSING THE WORLD OF DISASTER ASSISTANCE

The application process was itself no easy feat. Records of title, assessments, and taxes were lost in the floods. Every visit to the program offices and each new correspondence entailed re-introducing one's case to a stream of new officers assigned to their case, as if the program had no institutional memory of any work that had already been done.

VINCANNE ADAMS, *THE OTHER ROAD TO SERFDOM*

Making one's way as an exile was beset with more than the interpersonal and personal difficulties of finding a place to call a temporary home. The search for this place was confounded with the search for disaster assistance. Unleashed water would not be the only force to wreak havoc on the commonplace. For too many residents of this iconic city, the work of the many and varied government agencies and private contractors charged with responding to the disaster would generate a nightmarish world Kafka himself would recognize.[1]

"We tried to get rental assistance, but each time we thought we were close to getting it, someone would ask for another piece of paper we didn't have. We gave up."

"One day I think I'm going to get my FEMA trailer; the next day I don't know. What I don't know is more than I know."

"My house is flooded. I've lost everything, and a voice on the other end of the phone tells me I can't receive rental assistance without a copy of my last electric bill. Sweet Jesus, what planet is she from?"

"I can wade through water, but I can't wade through FEMA. Don't talk to me about FEMA!"

"I don't know who thought up the Road Home Program. It must have been an evil genius."

"I've fought for three years to get a fair settlement from Road Home. I can't figure out who is in charge there."

It wasn't supposed to be like this.

On September 16, 2005, President George W. Bush stood in New Orleans' famed Jackson Square. Behind him rose St. Louis Cathedral. With klieg lights ablaze he promised survivors of this catastrophic flood that help and perhaps humane change was at hand. In stirring words, Bush allowed that Hurricane Katrina might well be an opportunity to correct past wrongs and make a new, more just, city:

> Let us restore all that we have cherished from yesterday, and let us rise above the legacy of inequality. . . . When the streets are rebuilt, there should be many new businesses, including minority-owned businesses, along those streets. When the houses are rebuilt, more families should own, not rent, those houses. . . . And all who question the future of the Crescent City need to know: There is no way to imagine America without New Orleans, and this great city will rise again.[2]

It's no great stretch to imagine that those New Orleanians living throughout America in various states of evacuation and exile found some comfort in these words. If life on the road and life in search of place takes many unexpected turns and makes the unforeseen an unwelcome travel companion, President Bush's address offered hope that government knew how to help them remake their lives and their city. But, for those paying attention, another passage in his address foretold his administration's approach to this catastrophe:

> I challenge existing organizations—churches, Scout troops or labor union locals—to get in touch with their counterparts in Mississippi, Louisiana or Alabama, and learn what they can do to help. In this great national enterprise, important work can be done by everyone; and everyone should find their role and do their part.[3]

These words recall his father's famed "thousand points of light" call to civic responsibility. Encoded in President George H. W. Bush's trope and echoed in his son's address in Jackson Square is that clarion call that began with Reagan in the 1980s for the private sector do what the public sector will try hard to avoid. It is a philosophy of government whose animating principle is Hoover's version of "American individualism."[4] Bush junior's plea for "important work . . . by everyone" is a laudable entreaty, provided that it is founded on the public pledge that the resource of first recourse is a capable federal government willing to act. The stories told to us by residents of Hollygrove and Pontchartrain Park contradict any such vow.

While their accounts vary widely, together they tell a tale in which "everyone," each one, is more or less on his or her own. Lewis Carroll's Alice would likely find the worlds they describe much like her own. Like the craziness she sought to escape, far too many people seeking disaster assistance found themselves in a Wonderland listening to someone akin to the Doorknob who advises them: "Read the directions and directly you will be directed in the right direction."[5]

In chapters 3 and 4 we made the case that without some facility at improvisation, absent some skill in managing life in a makeshift way, staying reasonably sane in the aftermath of catastrophe would escape most of us. Floodwaters, evacuation, and exile demand the cleverness of the *bricoleur*, the jack-of-all-trades, the person able to make novel use of whatever resources are at hand. But there is some reason to expect that when a victim of disaster seeks assistance through a state or federal agency, the skills needed to navigate a program's demands would differ in kind from those required to stay afloat figuratively and at times literally during the emergency period.

A government program, after all, is routinely structured on a first-this-then-that logic, a linear order that moves in a more or less predictable direction, or so it would seem.

Catastrophe discloses a fundamental fact of human life, to wit: we need help, call it a higher worldly power, to survive. Needing what we cannot do for ourselves, we turn to this higher power, call it government, for protection and assistance. And herein begins a painful education for those who assumed a kind of social democracy was in place, capable and willing to provide the needed support. Under the most opportune political climate, however, the federal government is often less than up to the task of responding reasonably and humanely to catastrophe, and this was anything but a favorable political moment.

Michael Carrington from Pontchartrain Park, a voice we have encountered earlier, underscores the disconnect between the personal need for a higher power and the federal response to the flooding of the city.

"YOU ARE NOT REALLY HELPING"

We wondered, are we really in the United States? I don't know what country this is, really. The people who work for the government, they tell us, "We want to help you, come down here do this and that, fill this out." But what they are saying and what they are doing don't match. I said to myself, "You are not really helping." Telling me, "You have to do this and that and we can't help you until you do this and you don't qualify for this. This is not my responsibility." . . . I got real disgusted with what the government said they couldn't do when we've just had a catastrophe and need the government to do something. They are empowered to do things in a state of an emergency. Who was most empowered to help? The federal government. They've got the most resources and can respond to things most expeditiously if they so choose.

In ordinary times the actions of local, state, and federal governments might well be experienced as annoying if not downright exasperating and maybe, at times, as betrayal. But such actions are not likely to be seen as perilous. Low-probability, high-consequence events like Hurricane Katrina, however, are more likely to create long-drawn-out moments during which the work of the public sector to provide needed relief and assistance is itself a source of profound disorder and confusion, a kind of second disaster.

C. W. Mills counseled us to find the links between a personal trouble, the misery of one, and abstract, more impersonal forces that are likely creating the conditions for this trouble.[6] In this chapter we juxtapose personal stories highlighting the prominent role of the haphazard and the slapdash in the delivery of federal aid with our accounts of the logic of disaster-assistance policy and the politics of government relief in a historical moment favoring individualism over collectivism.

It is worth remembering that while disasters have occurred at least since the time of Noah, governments have not been in the disaster response business for all that long. Go back almost a hundred years from the flooding of New Orleans when, on a bright spring morning, another iconic American port city was almost completely destroyed.

AMERICA'S FIRST "MOST DEVASTATING DISASTER"

At 5:12 a.m. on April 18, 1906, the San Andreas Fault opened its craggy face and fired a potent shock of seismic energy. Its speed as it shot underground is estimated to have been seven thousand miles an hour.[7] Moments later, with a force greater than all of the explosives used in World War II, the quake ripped through the City by the Bay.

The earth fractured, and land reclaimed from marsh liquefied into a puddinglike substance. Vulnerable structures, brick and stone walls with no interior frames, simply collapsed. Wood- and steel-frame structures fared far better. Fires broke out around the doomed city. The fires would burn for three days, aided by the imprudent, some might say reckless, use of black powder to dynamite buildings ahead of the blaze. When on April 21 the last fires were extinguished, 514 city blocks, approximately 4 square miles, were incinerated. More than 29,000 houses and businesses were destroyed. In all, 80 percent of the city's 4.7 square miles was toppled or burned to the ground. Close to 90 percent of the city's 400,000 residents evacuated, many carrying only what they could throw in a bag or trunk. Estimates of deaths varied widely, between 700 and 3,000 or more.[8]

At the turn of the twentieth century there was no federal legislation in place to respond to the catastrophe in San Francisco. Andrew Carnegie donated $100,000, as did John Rockefeller's Standard Oil Corporation. London, England, contributed more than $300,000. Canada sent $100,000. Citizens in Oregon, Utah, Idaho, and elsewhere mailed loaves of bread to the city. Philanthropic relief efforts totaled more than $5 million.[9] Congress did approve $1 million for food, tents, and other tangible goods to be delivered to the city; President Theodore Roosevelt appealed to private donors for support. But this was the extent of the federal response to the worst urban disaster in the country's history.[10]

It would not be until 1950 that Congress passed the Disaster Relief Act, the first legislation authorizing a federal response to catastrophes in America. Its initial budget authorization was a mere $5 million, but it was a step in the direction of increasing the role the federal government was to play in disaster relief. It would take several more versions of this act before the federal government assumed its now-familiar role as the dominant material and financial responder to the nation's calamitous events.

ON FEDERAL DISASTER ASSISTANCE AND THE VAGARIES OF ELIGIBILITY

A significant change occurred in the 1969 recasting of the federal Disaster Relief Act that bears directly on how residents of Hollygrove and Pontchartrain Park experienced Hurricane Katrina. Responding to the impact of Hurricane Camille on the Gulf Coast and in Virginia and West Virginia, Congress passed Public Law 91-79:

> To provide additional assistance for the reconstruction of areas damaged by major disasters. Be it enacted by the Senate and House of Representatives of the United States of America . . . that Congress hereby recognizes that a number of States have experienced extensive property loss and damage as a result of recent major disasters including, but not limited

to, hurricanes, storms, floods, and high waters and wind driven waters and that there is a need for special measures designed to aid and accelerate the efforts of these affected States to reconstruct and rehabilitate the devastated areas.[11]

Public Law 91-79 expanded federal assistance to include town and city governments, but it also offered direct aid to private individuals. A historic distinction was drawn in this law between "PA" and "IA," shorthand for "public assistance" to rebuild infrastructure and "individual assistance" to rebuild the damaged lives of citizens.

Public assistance funding is provided to municipalities and states whose infrastructures are damaged by disasters. As of 2007, two years after Hurricanes Katrina and Rita finished their destructive journeys inland, federal funds accounted for more than 90 percent of repair work and removal of debris in New Orleans and along the Gulf Coast as well as inland.[12] A wide array of relief measures are funded under the IA initiative, among them emergency housing assistance, individual and family grants, food stamps, disaster unemployment payments, legal services, and crisis counseling.[13] Implementation of either program requires a presidential declaration of disaster.

There is one significant disparity between the PA and IA initiatives, however, that makes them quite unlike one another. Public assistance funding is provided without a determination that the civil authority receiving the funds meets certain criteria.[14] Once an affected county or parish is declared a disaster area, that legally designated unit is eligible for federal funds regardless of the socioeconomic status of the residents. Wealthy and impoverished towns alike are entitled to government assistance. Fisher Island, Florida, for example, with a per capita annual income in 2000 of $236,238, would be just as entitled to PA funding in the event of a declared disaster as would Allen, South Dakota, with a per capita income that year of $1,539.[15]

Individual assistance, IA funding initiatives, however, do require evidence of eligibility, at times an erratic and surprising array of such proofs. As straightforward as these requirements may sound to the uninitiated—Do you live in an officially declared disaster area? Has your house been damaged?—from the vantage point of those seeking IA support, the criteria for aid appeared to shift from one moment to the next. One neighbor would receive everything from FEMA, Red Cross, and even the Road Home Program, while another neighbor after numerous attempts would not receive anything at all.

A disconnect between making relief available and making it accessible haunted the efforts of people from both neighborhoods who sought help from the government. For those seeking IA support, the criteria for eligibility appeared to shift from one moment to the next depending on the day a call was made to seek assistance or check on a pending claim for help. Perhaps it depended literally on who you happened to speak with the day you were seeking assistance.

Clara Carrington of Pontchartrain Park recalls,

> Yes, we tried to get some money, but we didn't get a dime or a penny from FEMA or those other people, the Red Cross. We didn't get any help from the government while we were in Laplace. I really personally found Laplace . . . not open to helping us. Maybe I didn't get to the right people or something. But we didn't get any help. . . . They told us we had too much income to get rental assistance. They didn't give us anything, not a dime, and we went back twice because they told us to bring the receipts from the rent, bring receipts from utilities. We went twice and appealed and still didn't get anything. Other people did, I guess; it's whoever you have reviewing it. . . . [I]t's based on whoever you talk to, whoever is sitting at the desk or on the phone that decides what you get.

Another longtime resident of Pontchartrain Park, Alayna Millstone, recounts her somewhat bizarre encounter with FEMA:

> My first experience with the federal government was FEMA. Lady calls me, tells me she's calling me about the trailer, and she said, "How long will you need the trailer?" I said, "Honey, I don't know how long I'm going to need the trailer." So she says to me, "If you can't tell me how long you're going need the trailer, then I can't proceed." I said, "I think you people think this is a joke. I think the federal government needs to put all you FEMA employees on an airplane and bring you down here to New Orleans. And if you're reading from a script, that's a stupid question to be asking people in New Orleans 'cause nobody knows how long they're going to need a FEMA trailer." "Well if you can't tell me—" I said, "Okay honey, thank you, goodbye."
>
> I hung up the phone, and then I went into hysterics. I was at a laundromat with my sister, and she was like, "What's wrong with you?" I says, "I don't think we're getting a trailer." She says, "Why?" So I told her, and she said, "They'll probably call you back." When they didn't, she called them. My sister talked to them for months, and they turned her off . . . finally she told them off. And so, we never got a FEMA trailer, we never got any rental assistance.

Alayna reminds us that each life lived in disaster is one-off, singular, and tethered to social class:

You know, everybody's situation is totally different, unique. So you know, I don't know what people did to obtain the trailers. Maybe they didn't try. Maybe they tried and gave up. What is important day to day is to learn to pick and choose your battles. What battle are you going to fight today? What emotional turmoil do you want to go through? We are fortunate we had enough income that we could just go ahead and afford to rent a place and live as comfortably as we could. To be honest, we just gave up on FEMA.

If Alayna and her sister had successfully run this first gauntlet and qualified for a trailer, they soon would have discovered that more trials by fire awaited them. Once it was determined that a person qualified for a trailer, FEMA transferred the case to a private subcontractor responsible for bringing the trailer to the site. While the applicant could call the FEMA office to get an update on the delivery of the unit, it was nearly impossible to identify or contact the subcontractor. And once the trailer was delivered—and that could take weeks to months—a utility pole had to be installed. This required yet another subcontractor whose name and address often remained a mystery. Once the pole was in place, Entergy, the city's utility company, would have to install a transformer box to the pole connecting the trailer to the grid. It was anybody's guess when this step would occur. Finally, somebody somewhere needed to flip a switch to power up the trailer. Successfully negotiating this obstacle course could take months, and often did.

From shifting criteria of eligibility to the warren of unexpected turns and twists, people soon learned that there was no single discernible path to secure the disaster assistance that was, by all accounts, available. There was no predictable process to access this assistance. Everyone's path becomes his or her own. One person's experience could not serve as a blueprint for another. Each person seeking disaster relief would have little trouble finding a modicum of truth in Zarathustra's counsel to those in search of a better life:

This is my way; where is yours?
Thus I answered those who asked me "the way."
For *the* way, that does not exist.[16]

Hollygrove resident Kyneshia Mullens describes her search for a way to disaster assistance:

There are people who need the help, and it should be available for them but it is not always. I am not one to say that there are not programs out there that are there to help people. It's more of an issue of finding out about the programs and what they can do for you. We benefited from the help, but it was only because I had friends who called me from miles away to tell me, "Do you know such and such is available to help you with food and clothes or give you rental assistance?" I answered them, "No, I did not know that, but thank you for letting me know." And then I'd go and call my other friends and family members and tell them, and so on. . . . Especially for black families that is one of the main ways you survived in the past and are able to survive the hurricane right now, family support.

Tori Clarksdale is a resident of Pontchartrain Park. Her path differed from Kyneshia's. Each in its own way speaks volumes about the role of social capital in finding one's way through the looking-glass that was federal disaster assistance. A young mother of three, Tori describes her application for Road Home funding in an upbeat, almost celebratory manner:

It was easy for me. I applied early because my aunt . . . she's in real estate . . . was on the Road Home committee that was starting at our church. So I had a heads-up on what was kind of going on. So, she had given us the number in church, and she was like, "It's not out in the public yet, but this is the number to call to register." And I guess they went by first-come, first-served. I don't know how they did it, though. I called fairly quickly. I got my money fast, by March 2007. That's fairly quickly. See, I had applied in, like, March 2006. I got the second amount last year in December. The process was easy; it wasn't hard, because of my aunt, I believe.

It is worth noting that what Tori understood as receiving federal assistance "fairly quickly" was nevertheless thirteen months after initiating the application process. The place of human capital in accounting for how one pathway to assistance leads to success while another route fails is not hard to envision. But frequently, as we can see below, if the human providing assistance is also a victim of disaster, she might well find she has little personal reserve left to chart her own course to federal resources.

Pamela Harold describes the human assets needed to steer a course through the knotted skein of government assistance.

"IT WAS HARD FOR PEOPLE OF GOOD-THINKING MINDS TO TRY AND FIGURE IT OUT"

Well, the whole process was pretty interesting . . . I found that it took more than one person in a family to pull things together because it was so emotionally draining. You stayed on telephones with a lot of people . . . [Y]ou were misguided in a lot of situations. You couldn't find resources. The whole process took a collaborative effort to get it done. . . . [S]ome of the people on the phones were not nice to talk to, they were snappy, they were not understanding that you didn't have your policy. "Well, you know, I don't know my policy number, but I do know that this is the address." . . . "Well, I'm sorry, you need to . . . " "Lady, I just can't come up with this stuff."

So, they were very snappy, and I'm sure that a lot of them were working long hours and what have you, but it did not help people who were trying to get their lives back together. So I thought that initial process was really a very hard process. I thought that there was days when I was just emotionally tired, just tired. But there were days I knew the job had to get done, and I just had to work beyond that. And then, of course, you heard stuff, word of mouth. If you're standing in line at the Red Cross, somebody is talking about something you don't have, this or that document, and you go, "Oh no! I'm not going to get anything today." It was hard for people of good-thinking minds to try and figure it out.

I probably was one of the only people, I never got one cent from FEMA. I never got one cent from Red Cross. I never got any of those resources. It was like, I didn't care, I was gonna focus on getting my mother back together. I was like, "I'll be fine." You know, it was too hard to work on her stuff to think about my own stuff, so I just didn't care. I just knew that she just had to get back home, and she had to find some mental level here that could be at least enough for her to pull herself back together. So that process in itself, it was hard.

I mean, she was in an apartment; we ended up paying for it. We went to FEMA multiple times to say, "She is out of her home." And her insurance company did pay that little gap that they said that they would pay. But FEMA said they would pick up the rest. But we never got it. We filled out the paperwork at least five times. [Interviewer: You brought the same paperwork to FEMA five times?] Yes, the same paperwork five times. Plus the additional month's rent. [So, for almost three years, FEMA never paid the rent on your mom's apartment?] No, no. We never got a dime, never got a dime. You know, it's kind of like, "Okay, I just don't have energy to fight all these different systems."

Carolyn Chimes of Hollygrove found herself wandering through the confusing terrain of federal aid not only for herself but also for her parents and her aunt and uncle. Making calls to the many and varied official numbers to seek information, Miss Chimes often forgot on whose behalf she was advocating: "Was it my mom or my aunt today?" Also employed and needing to work while on her chimerical journey toward assistance, she adopted a novel and pragmatic strategy:

What I realized I had to do with all the FEMA mess, insurance, the whole nine yards, is to designate a day to fight. Because I couldn't fight every day; I couldn't do that. So I said on Wednesday, "It's on; I'm in war; I'm in battle all day. Wednesday from eight o'clock to six o'clock I'm in the fight." And after I got out of battle for that day, I had to rest because I noticed it was going to kill me, and that's not worth it.

An engineer employed by NASA, David Sawyer lives in Pontchartrain Park. The metaphor of the battle, of the fight, is also a part of his story as he sought the elusive Road Home assistance:

Yeah, there was a lot of waiting. You have to wait, wait, and you know, you have to wonder if you should accept what they offer you. Think we should have been told what to do and how to do it. But everybody we asked had a different story. Yeah, we didn't know that to get this money we would need to fight someone somewhere almost every day. I didn't know what I had to do. Well, I knew I had to fight. File some papers, go back, wait, get something from them asking for more papers or different papers, and then file some more papers. And while all this happens you're trying to keep your mind focused on getting your house back. You know, trying to get back to a stable life. But you got to fight.

In David's account we witness the standoff many residents faced: they on one side with this or that document or reasons for the difficulties in locating it and staff and administrators on the other side following today's interpretations of the rules—which might differ from yesterday's interpretations—regarding what documentation is necessary to be certified eligible for assistance. One lesson to take from this trouble is that IA resources might well be available, but at the same time, for too many people, the morphing vagaries of the eligibility criteria make it well nigh inaccessible. Summoning martial metaphors—fight, battle, war—to make sense of the quest for disaster assistance invites us to see how help itself can become a source of profound anxiety and fatigue, a second calamity, we might say.

INDIVIDUALISM TRUMPS COLLECTIVISM, FROM ROOSEVELT TO RAND

But the shifting evidence of eligibility is only the surface of this story, its most visible part. Disasters are never accidental events of history occurring outside the political, economic, and sociocultural drivers of the contemporary moment. It was the fate of people whose lives were upended by Hurricane Katrina to face catastrophe at a time when the place of government in the lives of U.S. citizens appeared as political novelist Ayn Rand might wish it to be. A New Deal–minded Franklin Delano Roosevelt, on the other hand, would find much to lament in twenty-first-century America. Three-quarters of a century earlier Roosevelt addressed the nation and uttered this to thunderous applause:

> We are determined to make every American citizen the subject of his country's interest and concern. . . . The test of our progress is not whether we add more to the abundance of those who have much; it is whether we provide enough for those who have too little.[17]

But by 2005, Rand's words rang louder and met with wider approval:

> The political philosophy of collectivism is based on a view of man as a congenital incompetent, a helpless, mindless creature who must be fooled and ruled by a special elite with some unspecified claim to superior wisdom and a lust for power.[18]

Rand's biting disgust for the virtues of social democracy is captured succinctly in a comment from the head of FEMA to a House subcommittee investigating the federal response to Hurricane Katrina. Questioned about the inability of his federal agency to get ice to citizens during the prolonged emergency period following the storm, Michael Brown answered bluntly, "I don't think that's a federal government responsibility to provide ice to keep hamburger meat . . . fresh."[19]

Michael Brown's arguably intemperate comment regarding ice, hamburger, and disaster was anticipated by his predecessor at FEMA, director Joe M. Allbaugh. In testimony to Congress regarding FEMA's upcoming 2002 budget, Allbaugh announced his chief priority: to reduce the federal agency's role in disaster mitigation and prevention. In his view, decisions about such activities were best left to state and local entities:

> It is not the role of the federal government to tell a community what it needs to do to protect its citizens. . . . Many are concerned that federal disaster assistance may have evolved into both an oversized entitlement program and a disincentive to effective state and local risk management.[20]

Efforts to miniaturize the federal role in response to Hurricane Katrina occurred simultaneously at several levels. A few days after his dramatic speech in Jackson Square, President Bush quietly issued an executive order suspending the Davis-Bacon Act requiring payment of prevailing wage rates and fringe benefits in federally financed or assisted contracts for construction or repairs in excess of $2,000. The secretary of Health and Human Services, Michael Leavitt, urged Senator Bill Frist and others to oppose a bipartisan emergency act to provide low-income disaster victims with Medicaid health coverage.[21] Republican Senator John Sununu articulated the administration's position: "We do not want to create a future economic catastrophe in our heartfelt efforts to deal with this natural disaster today."[22] Sununu's concern about creating an "economic catastrophe" apparently did not extend to sweetheart contracts.

Among the most egregious of the many misuses of federal dollars is FEMA's Operation Blue Roof. After all the proverbial palms were greased as money changed hands from the Shaw Group to one subcontractor after another, the average cost to put a blue tarp on a damaged roof was close to $2,500. This amount, in some cases, would just about cover the cost of a new roof.[23]

Anticipated by Rand more than fifty years ago and in arresting display by the testimonies of Allbaugh in 2002, Brown in 2006, and the political ma-neuverings of Leavitt, Frist, and Sununu is a seismic shift in the American political and economic landscape. In a perverse rendition of John Calvin, Rand, Allbaugh, Brown, Leavitt, and so on subscribe to some semblance of the idea that collectively we fail, individually we excel.[24] This idea is neatly captured in the history of the Road Home Program.[25]

Road Home is a federally funded plan to reimburse homeowners whose houses flooded when the levees—government-funded projects—crumbled in the wake of Hurricane Katrina. The plan was to supplement resources available from the National Flood Insurance Program by providing rebuild-ing grants to victims of the flood who did not have flood insurance. The plan would also provide supplemental assistance to cover the difference between flood insurance settlements and the cost of rebuilding or to buy flood-damaged houses at preflood market prices. Federal funds were sent to a newly created state office, the Louisiana Recovery Authority (LRA), to administer the program.

Rather than assume this responsibility itself or share it with FEMA, the state entered a no-bid contract with a private company, ICF International of Fairfax, Virginia, to run the program. The Inner City Fund (ICF) began more than fifty years ago as a venture-capital firm that financed inner-city businesses. ICF International was initially paid $756 million for its services. Approximately eighteen months later, the contract was amended, and the company's compensation jumped to $912 million.[26] One prescient observer of this move to privatize the administration of public relief wrote, "Humani-tarian relief and recovery assistance are now market affairs in which government remains, de facto, involved, but by way of markets organized for profit more than for relief."[27]

The process residents had to endure to receive this help moved at an excruciatingly slow and uneven pace, and it is safe to say that the program was a fiasco from the start. ICF did not have extensive experience in disaster administration and made many missteps while ramping up the program. Seventeen months after the flood, fewer than 500 of the initial 100,000 applicants had seen a nickel from the program.[28] Frank Silvestri was co-chair of the Citizens Road Home Action Group, a grassroots organization formed to represent homeowners struggling to get Road Home assistance. Silvestri said the company claimed to know how to administer such a program, "but what we've learned is it's been on-the-job training."[29]

One early problem was that ICF did not post rules for accessing Road Home funds on the Internet for a long time "for fear they would become a road map to fraud."[30] The presumption of larceny also informed requirements that applicants provide thumbprints along with the exhaustive list of difficult-to-obtain documents required for the application. In the end, 45 percent of 229,470 Road Home applications were either disqualified or denied support.[31]

For its part, ICF blamed the state's incompetence and the greedy behavior of disaster victims for its clumsy management of the program. A spokeswoman for ICF observed, "The state essentially redefined the goal of the program . . . in midstream." Channeling former FEMA director Joe Allbaugh, she worried aloud that the Road Home was viewed by those who lost their houses and possessions as an "entitlement program."[32] Raising the specter of moral hazard, it was thus incumbent on ICF International to vigilantly review every one of the applications to protect the government from fraud.[33]

Over the latter part of the twentieth century a collective-oriented, social-minded government was gradually displaced by a more limited, private-minded government. In this new model the public good is assured through market forces freed from government regulation in tandem with a high value placed on the pursuit of private gain. Success and well-being became singularly personal achievements in a way they were not from the 1930s through the 1970s.

The politics of limited government and competitive individualism might be of some value in the arena of the market, but when floodwaters reach your roof line and all you own is damaged or destroyed, when you and your family are pushed into exile and living on the limited goodwill of kin and friends or in hotel rooms or apartments, when your city is broken by catastrophe, small government and a firm belief that you are in control of your own fate are unlikely sources of comfort. Vulnerable, helpless, at times close to mindless, what people in these predicaments need most is properly organized, well-funded, and humanely delivered collective assistance. Assistance in this form, suffice it to say, was not forthcoming in the aftermath of the hurricane and flood.

MISS KATRINA MEETS FRANZ KAFKA

The disconnect between what victims of Hurricane Katrina needed and government response to those needs was expressed in striking prose by U.S. District Court Judge Richard Leon. Judge Leon responded to a case brought against FEMA by a nonprofit organization representing Katrina victims who were attempting to secure rental assistance while exiled from New Orleans. His order to FEMA was to "free these evacuees from the 'Kafkaesque' application they have had to endure."[34] His dictum might well stand as an iconic demand that all those seeking federal disaster relief meet with some semblance of common sense and fairness rather than a "nightmarishly complex, bizarre, or illogical" bureaucratic tangle, as Merriam-Webster's defines "Kafkaesque."[35] But common sense and fairness were not the drivers of the federal disaster response to Hurricane Katrina. For example, while the Road Home Program was ostensibly set up to assist homeowners, there was no comparable program to help renters, and this in a city where nearly half the residents rented. Eight years after the flood, 54 percent of renters in New Orleans are paying in excess of 35 percent of their pre-tax monthly incomes on rent and utilities. That marks a 43 percent increase since 2004.[36]

Perhaps Judge Leon had Rufus McDonald from Hollygrove in mind when he wrote his historic opinion. Mr. McDonald, a man of business, accustomed to the world of paper, found the incessant demands for more almost more than he could bear:

> I was telling my wife yesterday I was looking for some documents that the Road Home was asking for. They keep asking for other stuff I've done put it away because I'm through with it. I'd already given it to them once, files, a stack of receipts, and things. And I told them, "You know you got this stuff already." What is going on? I don't know how this works. All these receipts, and now I've got to go back through all this stuff again looking for something for them. But you've got to do it, and you wonder how you ever did it.

How might we, as students of society, approach demands like these—menacingly complex, chaotic, and all but sinister? How might we reason through a mad mix of putative regularity and happenstance? What would this sociology look like? More to the point, how would it help us make some reasonable sense of the accidental, fortuitous path taken by Jesse Gray to reach his goal of accessing Road Home assistance? Jesse's path is not something he would wish on anyone else, and yet it throws into stark relief a world of disaster relief bereft of reason and compassion.

"THIS WAS A DISASTER. I DON'T WANT TO TALK TO NO MACHINE"

I applied for Road Home money. I almost didn't get it, I guess. There was too much red tape. They would tell me, "You got to get this, got to get that." Like you needed your light bill, your last light bill, but all that's destroyed in New Orleans. Now you got to try and get a light bill, to show proof that you were staying in the house paying the light bill. . . . It's my house. I pay the bills. They tell you to call, you're calling, calling, you get the answering service, you're not talking to a human being, you're talking to a machine . . . it was rough. . . . This was a disaster. I don't want to talk to no machine.

We had a temporary FEMA office, and we would go talk to one of the representatives. They would tell me, "You have to get the deed to your house." Was it destroyed in the flood? I didn't know. I got lucky with the deed to my house. When I came back, when they let us back into the city, I had my deed in a cardboard suitcase. I found the suitcase, found my deed, so I let the sun dry it out. So I got lucky I had my deed. [Interviewer: You had them in a suitcase?] Right, the suitcase was full of water. My birth certificate and all that got destroyed. So I had to go all the way to Baton Rouge to get another birth certificate. Got there and the line looked ten miles long because everyone needed a birth certificate. Don't they know what flood can do to papers? Imagine if that deed had been destroyed. Man, oh, man! I doubt if I'd be sitting here now without that deed.

While all this is going on, my mother, she was in and out of the hospital. She suffers with congestive heart failure. I didn't know which way to turn. I bring her to the hospital, I bring her home, I go pick her up from the hospital, and after a while I take her back the same night. I got things like this going on when Road Home wants a copy of a light bill so I can get some money to rebuild my house? Every time I called they would tell me they're working on my case. The time was passing, passing, so I just gave up.

I told my wife, I said, "I'm going to put our house, this here house here for sale, whatever they give me for it, and we just going to rent." I was getting ready to sell this house and try to find me some property somewhere. And you know what? The day I was driving across the Huey P. Long Bridge to New Orleans to put a "for sale" sign in my yard, my phone rang. The woman on the other end was from Road Home. She had a settlement for me and asked me to come in. I couldn't hear so well because I was on top of the bridge, but that was the message.

That Road Home was too much. I didn't even apply for rental assistance. Trying to get the Road Home money and mother being sick, there was a lot going on.

One part of Jesse's story reads like a collection of miscellaneous contingencies. Lady Luck was with him: "So I got lucky I had my deed." But Mr. Misfortune was not far behind: "My birth certificate and all that got destroyed." Schopenhauer wrote that our lives "are somehow irresistibly shaped . . . by forces beyond our conscious will."[37] Perhaps Schopenhauer was thinking of disaster when he penned this line, perhaps not. But there is a way in which his words help us make sense of a part of Jesse's story, a telling that takes on a coherence in the recounting of one close call after another, right down to the last hour.

Confounding Jesse's struggle with the dueling uncertainties of luck and misfortune were the serial frustrations of trying to accommodate wildly fluctuating demands from anonymous voices representing a massive federal and private bureaucracy. Jesse knew that Road Home funding was available and promised homeowners like him a new start, but the perplexing confusion that was the Road Home Program made accessing this resource itself a source of abiding stress and uncertainty. Jesse might have wondered if the program's representative who asked him for a copy of his last electric bill might be posing a riddle. To someone like Jesse who evacuated just ahead of the flood and was now living in exile, the question "Do you have a copy of your last electric bill?" might have sounded deliberately misleading.

En route to put his house up for sale, Jesse got the call from Road Home, turned his car around, and headed back to his place in exile pondering how he would restore his home rather than sell it. At the end of Jesse's trip through Alice's Wonderland that was Road Home, he received money to rebuild. The sum he was promised was the sum he received. That did not always happen, however. More than a few residents found themselves at journey's end dog-tired but pleased that, at last, money to rebuild would be forthcoming—only to discover that their checks from Road Home were substantially less than they had agreed to. Forced back on the path, they found themselves in one more fight.

Alayna Millstone gives an account of her experience with the federally sponsored, privately administered program.

"IN THE END WE GOT SOME ROAD HOME MONEY BUT NOTHING TO WRITE HOME ABOUT"

All I can tell you is God bless Road Home. And that's as far as I'm gonna go—because I don't want that on tape; Road Home was not very nice. I wouldn't wish that program on nobody. Back and forth, forth and back, talking to one person that said this, and then the next one said that, and that didn't correspond with what the first person said. Then you had to start the process all over again. We filled out one paper, the first day, and then we went back, and they said, "Oh, that wasn't the right form. You have to fill out another form," and you had to bring this with you. But I didn't have it. So there I had to go back to my place and start all over again. And then when I returned the next day with the paper the person told me that she couldn't file anything because she was just an information person and not authorized to file paperwork.

But as happened with Jesse, after a seeming time without end, a call came. A settlement was at hand. Alayna and her sister drove to the Road Home office, more than a little elated that their rocky path to federal assistance was at an end. When examining the final paperwork, however, they were stunned:

When we looked at the paper with our settlement number on it, the amount was totally different than the sum we were promised. It was a good deal less than what we were told. My sister had a meltdown. So we rescheduled to go back, I don't know, a week later, three weeks later, you lose track of time.

When we went back the second time, the amount was even less than it was the first time we looked at it! At that point, I was emotionally spent. I put it in the Lord's hands. I didn't even file an appeal because I just didn't want to deal with the federal government anymore. In the end we got some Road Home money but nothing to write home about.

Alayna is a graduate of Tulane University, a smart, knowledgeable, middle-class professional. We might imagine that she would have the skills to chart a course through the maze of federal and private bureaucracies to get what she needed to begin the next test facing her: rebuilding her damaged house. It is one thing to navigate uncharted terrain that is fixed, relatively unchanging; it is quite another to steer a course through a landscape that appears this way one day and another way the next. When an agreed-upon settlement for Road Home funding morphs into another number and again into yet another number with no apparent reason, it is likely to render whatever skills and resources one brings to the table less than helpful. The wild swings from no money to money, as in Jesse's case, or the baffling surprise at the end of the journey when the amount promised is suddenly cut substantially and then cut again, are the kinds of disorienting events that kept people off balance, unsure, and over time, used up. But there is a back-story to Alayna's trials and tribulations with Road Home, one worth telling.

ROAD HOME AND RACE

In 2008 the Greater New Orleans Fair Housing Action Center, National Fair Housing Alliance, and five African American homeowners filed a class-action lawsuit in the U.S. District Court for the District of Columbia against HUD and the Louisiana Recovery Authority. The suit alleged that the LRA's Road Home program discriminated against African American homeowners in New Orleans. The suit points out that the formula to calculate grants used the prestorm value of residents' houses rather than using actual estimates of rebuilding costs. As a consequence, black moderate- and low-income homeowners received less money than their mostly white counterparts living in comparably built and equally damaged but higher-valued homes in predominantly white neighborhoods. The suit stated that the grants from Road Home should be based on rebuilding a house rather than on the prestorm value of that house. In July 2011 HUD and the LRA changed the Road Home program grant formula to provide full relief to more than 13,000 homeowners. All eligible low- and moderate-income homeowners—mostly African Americans in New Orleans—received un-capped additional compensation grants totaling approximately $473 million based on the estimated cost of damages to their houses and not the lower prestorm market value of those houses.[38]

While courts belatedly salvaged some of the miscarriages of disaster assistance, Alayna and her sister, Jesse, Clara, Pamela, David, and so many others found the work of obtaining federal assistance exhausting, requiring each day what William James once called "the slow dull heave of the will."[39] And in the end, millions of dollars in federal disaster relief for survivors of Hurricane Katrina remained unspent. One way of making some sense of this anomaly is to assume that thousands of people who might well have been eligible found themselves, after so many maddening efforts to access the help, unable to muster one more heave of the will to face the muddle that was disaster assistance.

"WHY IS A RAVEN LIKE A WRITING DESK?" OR "DO YOU HAVE A COPY OF YOUR LATEST ELECTRIC BILL?"

The unreal can be a powerful illustration of the real. We might imagine for a moment that we are straddling two worlds, one fictional, the other factual. The fictional world is the scene from *Alice's Adventures in Wonderland* when the Mad Hatter is posing a riddle to the Doormouse, the Hare, and Alice.[40] In the factual world is a survivor of Miss Katrina now living in exile who is seeking rental assistance. Speaking to Alice, the Mad Hatter asks, "Why is a raven like a writing desk?" Speaking to the survivor, the Road Home representative poses this question or riddle, if you will, "Do you have a copy of your latest electric bill?" The survivor, like Alice, puts her mind to work. "Is this a puzzle, a riddle, how do I answer this question?" Moments later the survivor asks, "Why do you ask me for this one document when you know my house and all I own was flooded, when you know that in leaving my house to escape the water the whereabouts of my electric bill was not on my mind?"

It is worth noting that when pressed to explain his own riddle, the Hatter admits, "I haven't the slightest idea." In the Hatter's response Carroll creates a wildly absurd moment that might well stand for the experiences of too many survivors of Hollygrove and Pontchartrain Park who sought the help President Bush promised that day in early September 2005.

REBUILDING IN A BROKEN CITY

Each of the last three chapters is an inquiry into how people in two New Orleans neighborhoods pushed back against the autocracy of chance. If our quotidian lives are spent working to stand upright in the shifting terrain of order and disorder, those whose stories we have recounted thus far might be said to have unwittingly found their feet slip-sliding in the muddle and confusion that was Hurricane Katrina. For each of them the sum of most if not all things nonsensical somehow had to be reasoned with. As we saw, many people drove themselves relentlessly to regain a foothold in a world where recurrence and prediction could once again compete with their opposites.

One major and arguably last task faced most residents of Pontchartrain Park and Hollygrove: rebuilding their flood-damaged houses. A daunting task, no doubt, but one that need not, on the face of it, be as contingency-ridden as the previous challenges they faced. After all—relative to all that had happened to them up to now—how dependent on the unforeseen is putting up drywall, rewiring, plumbing, and so on? Concrete tasks, one and all. But the hunt for solid footing, a terra firma, was not over for them. This, their next trial, typically began with a first look at what two weeks of six to eight feet of stinking, chemical-laced water can do to a house.

FIRST SIGHTINGS

Pamela Harold remembers what she saw and felt when she returned to her house in Hollygrove once the floodwaters retreated:

> I guess you could say I just walked to the door and peeked in. I just can't explain how I was feeling. It just hurt so bad, you know? Nothing you could save. The whole thing was a dumpster. The refrigerator lying on the middle of the floor, and I said, "How can water do this?" Something

just happens in your mind. It just was not my house; it was just a shell to come back to.

David Sawyer is an engineer who works for NASA in Mississippi and lives in Pontchartrain Park. David is accustomed to a world of precision and order. Setting eyes first on his neighborhood and next on his house—where seven to eight feet of water once lapped at his roof for the better part of two weeks—it looked to him as if a nuclear winter had replaced the usual sun of late summer. He saw death:

> When I first came in the neighborhood to look at the house, to me it was like a bomb, just like an atom bomb. Everything was gray, shades of gray. Horrible is what it was, no birds, no nothing. And when I came up to the house and opened the door, kind of pushed the door open, I saw it. It was almost like your life flashed in front you. It was like, everything you, you know, you worked for, everything you had. It must be like when you die.

Denise Anders drove the eight or nine hours from Tyler, Texas, with her son to see her house in Hollygrove:

> We pull up to the front of the house. . . . I can see the residue or water line on the glass door. I said, "Richard, everything we have and everything in this house is materialistic. If there's not anything left, remember it was a loan from God; whatever is gone is gone. . . ." So we walked in the house. The residue line was like four feet high. There's black mold and mildew from the floor all the way to the ceiling. The only thing that was alive was his Russian tortoise, Chopper. It was still in the tank; it must have floated. Chopper was still alive. So we got Chopper, two pairs of shoes and a hat . . . I'm thinking, "Get me out of here."

Chopper the turtle survived; he could swim.

Tori, a single mother living in Pontchartrain Park, opened the door to her flood-ravaged home and set her eyes on a lone table still standing in her kitchen:

> The two rabbits were on the table because we left the rabbits home. We were gone for two months. Oh, my goodness it was so graphic. We had let them out so they could get to food and stuff. They were on the table. They hopped up there. That was the highest spot they could get to. They drowned.

Pamela, David, Denise, and Tori each gazed on what was at one time a home; they could make little sense of what lay before them. What was once familiar and certain was now just beyond recognition, a transfixed moment of appalling surprise. For many, their houses became monuments to despair. There was much to do.

During the time of rebuilding, some lived in FEMA trailers, others hunkered down in their damaged houses, some lived in cars or trucks, still others drove hour upon hour to work on their houses only to return to their places in exile late at night. All had multiple "folders" open at once, projects aplenty that had to be completed. Adding inestimably to their mission was the blunt reality that they would have to accomplish it in what could only be described as a broken city, partnered with ineffective state and federal disaster administrations determined to turn disaster relief into an exercise in personal autarky. If we could imagine a mantra for this next test of human character on their long slog home, it might sound something like the refrain from Jackson Browne's "The Pretender," who, knocked down but not out, shouts, "I'll get up and do it again. Amen. Say it again."[1]

A CITY IN A COMA

A reporter for the *Times-Picayune* assessed the pace of urban restoration a calendar year from August 29, 2005, the day Miss Katrina slapped New Orleans' east side. She likened the city to being in a coma.[2] She cites an economist from Moody's investment firm who noted, "This is the first time in U.S. history where a city has sat dormant for almost a year."[3]

By August 2006, only 16 percent of the city's buses were in use. Forty percent of the urban electric grid was still down, and 60 percent of residents who either stayed through the flood or returned after were unable to hook up to the natural gas grid. While 80 percent of the hotels had reopened, 50 percent of the city's medical facilities were still closed.[4] In late 2008 an MIT report on the rebuilding of the city described it as "devastatingly slow," noting that much of the destruction wrought by the flood remained as it was in "the immediate aftermath of Katrina." Three years after the flood, recovery was "placed on the shoulders of neighborhoods and citizens, without providing them the means to achieve their goals."[5]

But the glacial pace of infrastructure recovery was only a symptom—albeit a critical one—of the underlying malady: the absence of anything approaching a coherent urban recovery plan connected in any sensible way to the allocation of rebuilding assistance. Tulane historian Lawrence Powell depicts in blunt words the failure of the mayor and City Council in the face of historic destruction. "The city," he writes, "has made a hash of post hurricane planning, and the invisible hand of the market is raising its middle finger."[6] Amy Liu, deputy director of the Brookings Institution's Metropolitan Policy Program, and her colleagues on the Katrina Index project are blunt in their own manner, noting that before the city had a chance at recovery it would "need to have a functioning government with a reliable and decent delivery of services."[7] What Liu and her colleagues could not know was that nine years after Hurricane Katrina flooded the city, C. Ray Nagin, then mayor of the city, would be sentenced in federal court to ten years in prison for, among other things, contractor fraud in allocating federal dollars for rebuilding. A functioning government was not in the city's foreseeable future.[8]

New Orleans' troubled municipal response to the flooding of the city is brought to life in Cheryl's animated account of her trip to a City Council meeting.

"SO LET'S NOT BLOW SMOKE . . . I JUST CAME TO SAY YOU CAN GO TO HELL"

There was this stage after the hurricane where there wasn't a single piece of accurate information. We heard rumors, we heard numbers we could call and things that we could do, the things that might be happening. We had the elevation requirements and we had the decisions by some unknown entities about the criteria for declaring our houses damaged to this or that degree. If our homes were declared more than 50 percent damaged, then we had this mystical elevation requirement. If our homes were 80 percent damaged we had another magical requirement. In this neighborhood, the elevation requirement was to raise the house three feet, and as you can see from my waterline monument there, three feet would still have put us in a wading pool. . . . I was declared 48 percent damaged; for whatever reason you were declared 48 percent damaged. It was a supernatural evaluation of 48 percent.

I went to the City Council meeting to find out if there was still going to be an elevation requirement, because Pontchartrain Park is a historic neighborhood, was it was going to be bound to those same elevation requirements? I got there early, I parked four blocks away, I walked and sat in my little seat at the City Council. I listened to Councilman Oliver Thomas and that preachy woman from East New Orleans who should be a reverend and not a City Council member talk about what has happened and what we're not going to stand for, but they did not have a single piece of useful or technical information.

And, there were people swimming about with little cards, where you could write your name and where you were from and what your question was and you could ask this question if they called your name. So I wrote down a question and I wrote my name, and somewhere around the third, fourth, or fifth person they called my name, and I walked up there, and they asked, "What is your question?" And I said, "Well, you know what my question is because you had to approve the question before I came up here because you read the little index card. So let's not blow smoke, I'm not in the mood. I just came to say you can go to hell, the president can go to hell, the mayor can go to hell, and the governor can go to hell, and I'm going home." Oliver Thomas said, "I understand how you feel."

And I said, "You really shouldn't say that because you don't know how I feel. You don't know who I am. You don't know what it took me in my life to become a homeowner. You don't know about my nightmares. You don't know about my fears and my insecurities. You don't know how unprepared I am for the disaster that I am living. So please don't tell me you understand."

I told them that I was disappointed because I expected and the three hundred people in the room expected information and they expected help, and they expected to go away comforted. I said, "I don't need a bitch session, I'm a grownup. I don't need you to vent. What I need is for you to do your jobs. If there's something you can do to help the citizens, I'd love to hear it. Otherwise I'm going it alone. I see no reason to continue to pay $5 an hour to park. That's it." And I left. The next day I began the process of rebuilding my home.

The New Orleans City Council appeared to Cheryl about as confused and confounded by Miss Katrina as the three hundred or so people in the council chamber, perhaps more so. The palpable confusion among City Council members originates, no doubt, from several sources, not the least of which is a long city history of government mismanagement. But more was going on than just the past made present. Take, for example, what might be called "the elevation grant game."

An increasingly popular mitigation strategy for Louisiana homeowners is to elevate their houses. A raised house was at a lower risk of flooding. It sounds simple. But this funding came much slower than the Road Home money to repair houses, leaving people in the uncomfortable spot of having to rehab their houses before elevating them, or wait for funding while living in a FEMA trailer, renting or living off the good will of others.

For not a few residents, the cost of elevating their houses exceeded the monies allowed for the construction. Some people elevated their houses before renovation with money left over after they paid the balance on their mortgages. The transparent absence of coordination between funding for elevation and Road Home's housing rehab grants confused and frustrated an already stressed population. For its part, the City Council appeared at least as confused as the residents themselves on this matter.[9]

The inability to rely on municipal or federal authorities to guide the herculean task of rebuilding two-thirds of the city and the ensuing need to take matters into one's own hands is also expressed in this short account from Jo Johnston, who lives two streets over from Cheryl.

"SO WE GOT AN ATTITUDE"

My grandmother had this house blessed when we first moved in here. Her name was Florence Mary Earl Johnston. And we knew we was coming back home. That wasn't a question. We heard of all the rumors—they were going to make green space and a couple other things. And we said, "No, we're going back home." . . . [W]e heard that you had to elevate, and they were going to tear down everything. It went from rumor to rumor to rumor. And we started looking at the news and we said, "Okay, they're not making the commercial buildings file a such-and-such, so why should we file a such-and-such?" So we got an attitude. And we said, "We're going home to fix up our house." And we did.

Cheryl's and Jo's frustration at the futile search for answers from city officials about rebuilding mirrors the experiences of many New Orleanians. An understaffed city permits and inspection department was charged by FEMA with deciding if homes were "substantially damaged"—more than 50 percent of prestorm house value—and required elevation or other flood mitigation measures before permits were issued to repair the buildings. While a determination of substantial damage could slow rebuilding, it potentially provides access to an increased cost of compliance (ICC) grant of up to $30,000 under the NFIP Hazard Mitigation Grant Program.[10]

But it was not clear in early 2006 what elevation standard FEMA would apply to this disaster and how that would affect rebuilding. In addition, the federal government refused the State of Louisiana's plan to use Hazard Mitigation Grant funds as part of the Road Home Program, which delayed allocation of elevation grants. What emerged was an ass-backward process in which the allocation of rebuilding funds poorly matched the needs of those doing the rebuilding.

There was very little that amounted to precision in the city's damage-determination process, as decisions were typically based on elevation maps and prestorm house values without visual inspection of the residences. Appeals of initial damage assessments were frequent as people tried to figure out what "substantially damaged" meant and how it was determined. Some appeals required certification of damage and elevation from an engineer, while other appeals were worked out, after long waits at city hall, with clerks from the city permits office without any written evidence. It was nothing if not fickle, and many people gave up on the process.

Adopting the stance of "We are just going to do it," whether local or federal authorities know what they are doing or not, is a subtext of the dozens of stories we were told in the course of this study. Going it alone did not mean going without the aid of family and friends. It did not mean that volunteer groups and organizations were not there to lend a hand; they were. Going it alone, in this context, describes the disconnect between the needs of citizens and the readiness or capacity of governments to respond in a meaningful and intelligible manner to those needs.

With upward of two-thirds of the housing stock in New Orleans damaged in the flood, the city faced a task of historic proportions. The scale of this massive urban reconstruction was paralleled only by the San Francisco earthquake and fire of 1906. Reason might well suggest that city government, perhaps in tandem with the state, would create and implement a transparent program for assisting homeowners in the arduous task of rebuilding their houses and neighborhoods. But neither federal, state, nor New Orleans municipal authorities were able to create such a program. What was created only added to the surreal experience following Hurricane Katrina.

The city's first comprehensive reconstruction plan, Bring New Orleans Back, was funded by a real estate developer and written largely by the Urban Land Institute. Ed Blakely, a city planner and academic, was appointed to implement the plan. Without a hint of hubris, he likened his task to that of Andrew Jackson, who led his troops in battle against the British in a failed attempt to capture New Orleans in January 1815:

> I arrive in New Orleans on January 7, 2007, the 192nd anniversary of the historic Battle of New Orleans. I had been called to take command in a new and perhaps more daunting battle for the life and soul of the nation's most distinctive city. This was my first official day on the job as the "czar" to lead the post–Hurricane Katrina recovery effort.[11]

Well before arriving, Blakely had promised the city that it would soon see industrial "cranes in the sky" and a new and greatly improved New Orleans. In the end, however, this plan is best remembered for the green dots placed on planning maps of the city. These dots designated planned future green spaces where once vital neighborhoods now stood ravaged by flood damage. The immediate problem was, simply, that most residents fully intended to rebuild their houses in these neighborhoods. Historic neighborhoods like

Broadmoor and parts of Mid-City, Lakeview, and New Orleans East were slated for demolition.[12] Public outcry shouted down this plan and warned off any local leader who planned to solicit federal Hazard Mitigation funds to buy blocks of blighted property through the Road Home Program.

Blakely blamed his difficulties in implementing an effective recovery strategy by referring "to the city's racial factions as 'a bit like the Shiites and Sunnis,'" calling "the civic elite 'insular,' and" observing that "the newcomers he wants to draw here will be impatient with local 'buffoons.'" Blakely quit his position in 2009 and returned to Australia, about as far from New Orleans as one can get.[13]

A second initiative turned the planning process over to a local charity, the Greater New Orleans Foundation, GNOF. The GNOF received a grant totaling $3.5 million from the Rockefeller Foundation. Planning teams were created. Displaced residents and those who had returned were encouraged to attend meetings to talk about how to rebuild their houses and neighborhoods. Mayor C. Ray Nagin described the process as "democracy in action."[14]

The problem with his vibrant democracy trope, however, was first, it was philanthropic and not an exercise in the power of the polis. While charity might be a critical part of any society, the rebuilding of New Orleans would require massive state and federal assistance, both financial and technical. This assistance was very slow to materialize. Second, it was difficult for people in many neighborhoods to attend the planning sessions. With some people still in exile, others living in chloroform-contaminated FEMA trailers,[15] and still others squatting in abandoned housing, most all of them battling to get some disaster assistance, it was difficult to create viable grassroots groups that could honestly be said to represent their neighborhoods. Mounting confusion about damage assessments, Road Home, and the planning process all fueled the chaos and the go-it-alone attitude about rebuilding.

Returning residents like Cheryl learned quickly that they would have to step up and remake their own houses and neighborhoods. Although the *New York Times* is not a widely read newspaper in New Orleans, homeowners in both neighborhoods probably would nod knowingly to an article that appeared in it more than a year after the flood—"In New Orleans, Each Resident Is Master of Plan to Rebuild." The reporter provides a couple of examples of going it alone worth citing here:

> In the Holy Cross area, one of the few sections of the Ninth Ward that was not washed away by the storm, a handful of residents are fashioning street signs by hand because the city has yet to replace any. Across the city, in

Lakeview, a group of homeowners have been seeking corporate sponsors and even selling T-shirts to raise money to rebuild a fire station, since they discovered that they cannot take out fire insurance without one.[16]

As we sort through the ways social class shaped the lived experience of disaster, there is some value in noting that the average annual household income in the Holy Cross neighborhood in 2000 was $32,202, while the average householder in Lakeview earned $63,984.[17] Residents of flooded neighborhoods, across the class spectrum, were going it alone. We should acknowledge that a family going it alone with twice the income of another family forced to make its own way is likely to encounter a materially different journey.

There were many publicly funded efforts to aid the rebuilding, but their requirements were not transparent to many citizens. For example, hundreds of millions of federal dollars were allocated to selected national contractors to haul away the waterlogged and mold-stained possessions of hundreds of thousands of New Orleans residents. Those at the top of the contracting pyramid like Philips-Jordan and the Shaw Group did not typically pick up debris; they hired tiers of subcontractors to do the job. A road-grading company from Florida with heavy equipment and connections with a top-tier contractor came to New Orleans to pick up the detritus of disaster.[18] Adding to the gaggle of corporate-paid subcontractors were the itinerant "gypsy" contractors who competed each day with local laborers.

Wayne Lerner from Hollygrove adds a personal voice to the description of the disjointed efforts to fix a broken city:

> Another thing that kind of pisses me off is that this happened to the natives of New Orleans. This storm happened to us. We should be training our own young men to learn a building trade. Instead, people that are not from here are getting all of this work and our young people are not getting any of it. There's nothing here, no kind of programs to teach any of these young guys the skills to give them jobs that need doing. Everything seems backwards. It seems like the city should be helping us and they are not. It seems like they should be cleaning the city up and they are not. Volunteers are cleaning up the city; our government's not doing it.

Mr. Lerner looks at the ruin all about him and wonders how local and federal government officials could not see what needed to be done and, using local workers, get about the business of effectively doing it. Perhaps a local Job Corps program, perhaps a clearinghouse for contractors to submit their licenses for approval before hauling debris or working on houses, would have been appropriate.

The inability of the City of New Orleans to design and implement a sustainable urban revitalization strategy precluded the possibility that a municipal authority would be appointed to oversee and arbitrate problems between building contractors and homeowners. Absent this official ombudsman resource, homeowners throughout the city found themselves in yet another uncertain world, tasked with making some sense out of the seeming senselessness of it all. Not surprisingly, the city quickly flooded with itinerant contractors who sought to capitalize on the construction boom. Some were skilled; some were not.

Contractors had more clients than they could serve; construction crews were quickly assembled and reassembled. It appeared as if every other journeyman assumed the title "contractor," while every other helper claimed to be a "journeyman." People stormed the limited building-supply stores looking for lumber, electrical and plumbing fixtures, stoves, and refrigerators. Supplies were limited. Lines were long. Nerves were frayed.

And lest we forget, many homeowners faced the crazy quilt of contractors while living great distances from New Orleans. Denise Anders tells this story.

"I'M NOT TAKING ORDERS FROM A FEMALE"

When I was fixing up my house I would leave Tyler, Texas, on Friday and get here Friday night. I would do what I needed to do with the contractors on Saturday. Sunday midday I would leave and be back in Tyler late Sunday night. I had a job I had to be to on Monday.

The first time I came back to work on the house, my friend had a bunch of contractors meet me at the door. And when they saw that I was a female and I'm telling them I want this done, that done, and so on, they were like, "No, no, I'm not taking orders from a female." So they left. So I'm crying and praying. I can't do this. How am I going to find somebody?

Another friend of mine recommended some other contractors. "They cost a little more, but they are good," he said. I said, "Bring them." So I came back down on Friday and Saturday, maybe five or six of his guys show up. By Sunday before I left the house was framed how I wanted it. They spoke Spanish and I was like, "I don't know what y'all talking about, but y'all working like I don't know what." I needed that.

So I had this routine. I would come from Tyler on Friday after work and buy material. But it was scary. I'm buying this material, and I get back to the house and I'm like, I'm the only one on this street. And the house has no windows. And I have like $5,000 worth of material. The guys wouldn't show up until Monday or Tuesday. So I'm crying, "Lord don't let nobody go in here." I did have a gate then. I locked it and prayed. I can close the door but I can't lock it, and the windows are totally gone. But no one stole anything.

One weekend I came down and bought $3,000 worth of windows. I had to leave them in the house on Sunday to drive back to Tyler. My friend said, "Just do that whatever you Catholics do, sign the cross and pray." No one touched anything; no one stole anything from my house. Nothing was ever missing. It was the end of May 2006 when I started work on the house. And we were back in the house the first week of August, just about a year from the hurricane.

But Denise's worries were not yet over:

We were back but nobody else was on our street. I wondered who is coming back, who is not coming back. I prayed because I'm in a house with no phone service. A year after the storm and the lines were still dead. I don't think I had a phone until November. So it was just me and my son; no one was back but us. I'm praying, "Lord, how is this going to work?" Finally, we got phone service. I was able to get an alarm system. I need these things. It is almost three years since Hurricane Katrina, and I'm still here by myself.

A single mother living more than eight hours from New Orleans was faced with the near-epic task of arranging for the reconstruction of her house while working a full-time job in exile to make ends meet. Three years after the storm, she was the only person on her street to have returned. More would come, but Denise was the pioneer.

Wayne Lerner was thirty-two years old when the city flooded. He had lived in Hollygrove for two years.

"OH WELL, JUST KILL ME, THEN"

I have a family house on Palmetto Street. I got back to the city in January 2006. I had no place to live, but I knew I had to fix up my house. So, I lived in my truck parked in front of my house. I slept in the truck. Sometimes I would sleep in the house. I had no running water or power. I was isolated. There was no one on the block but me at this time. No one came around. It was just me and my guitar.

So, I'm a carpenter. I'm a tradesman. I was able to get odd jobs to survive. I had transportation. If you had a vehicle, especially a truck, you could make money moving debris. I did manage to do some odd jobs to make money and to eat and to take care of myself while I worked on my

6.1. Denise's rebuilt house in Hollygrove surrounded by vacant lots, 2010. Photo by Amanda Figueroa.

house. I worked for a few contractors. It's funny, you have people that became contractors after Katrina; they weren't contractors before. A lot of people have gotten stiffed with some really bad work.

Then I got stiffed working for some of them. You work a whole week with a guy and he disappears on payday. Since the storm, that's happened to me about four times. I could either find this person and do them something or forget about it. I just licked my wounds and went about my business. I had to rebuild my house.

But it makes me real mad because I know that there are people that still owe me money and I see them almost every day. I seen a guy the other day, I said, "Hey what's your reason for not paying me? Just tell me, What is your reason for not paying me?" His name is Jerome. I said, "Jerome, man, look, what if I'm a violent person? You don't really know me. What if I was some crazy person and you haven't paid me yet?" He said, "Oh well, just kill me then." I just looked at him and walked off.

Mr. Lerner summed up his interview with us this way: "As far as I'm concerned I have no story; I'm just talking about my experience." For him, "story" is fiction, something made up. The predatory world he describes was anything but imaginary. The palpable greed and lawlessness that emerged during the rebuilding phase of this disaster reflects in part the absence of a municipal authority governing the relationships between contractors and homeowners.

Like the working-class neighborhood of Hollygrove, the middle-class neighborhood of Pontchartrain Park was also an often volatile site, pitching homeowners against contractors. Cheryl contrived a unique if arguably dangerous strategy.

"AND IF THEY TRY TO PULL AWAY I TRY TO HIT THEM WITH MY CAR"

I know that there's this mysterious disappearing act performed by electricians, plumbers, and drywallers. So we decide on the price and decide when they were coming. And the understanding was, they would be working here every day. So I would pay them and then they would think I would leave, but I go down on the corner and I wait there for twenty minutes. And if they try to pull away I try to hit them with my car. And I would block them and honk at them with my horn and harass them right to the next location that they were going to and make it completely impossible for them to do their jobs elsewhere because they are supposed to be here, and they are supposed to be here every day.

And I dated a policeman who tracked down everyone's home address. I'd go to their house bright and early in the morning and say, "Okay, chop chop! Got to get your booty to my neighborhood and work on my house." And so I did that. The longest stretch that there was no work on the house was eleven days. But it took all my energy and time to keep them working.

Cheryl, in the end, prevailed.

Joseph Shearman lived in Hollygrove all his life. He was determined to return to New Orleans and rebuild his house. He did not expect that he would be caught in the middle of a violent altercation between contractors.

"I CALLED 911"

I'm really blessed. . . . I made sixty-five yesterday. Monday, I went to criminal court to testify against a contractor who smacked one of his workers on the head with a board right on my porch. I called 911. That was the end of that contractor. The guy I went to testify against was the sheetrock contractor and did the windows and the sheetrock. When this happened, the guy he hit was a finisher and he was in here finishing up the sheetrock. I had to fire the finisher too. The guy who got hit was Hispanic. The guy who hit him was black. He pleaded guilty and plea-bargained to a misdemeanor assault. I got a house to fix and these guys are trying to kill one another.

6.2. Cheryl's rebuilt house in Pontchartrain Park, 2014. Photo by Heather Huey.

In these vivid passages Wayne, Cheryl, and Joseph bring to life the chaotic and sometimes violent world of rebuilding in a city devastated by a massive flood and missteps at every level of government. Not surprisingly, in this confusion and disorder, quality—getting the job done right—was in short supply. Some contractors were, simply, unskilled and unlicensed. Others hurried one job to get to the next. Kylee Grimm, a longtime resident and historian of Hollygrove, tells her rebuilding story.

"WE FOUGHT THE BATTLE OF THE CONTRACTORS"

I got one contractor. He told me, "I can have your house done in three months." I said, "Good, I'll give you your money in three months." Oh, no, he wants money on this day, then money on that day; it was all hit and miss. We fought the battle of the contractors.

He was supposed to level the house and he didn't. He got it to the studs and he did the electrical, but he did such a poor job of it. Like in this room I have to flip this switch, flick that switch, come back and flick the other switch for the lights to come on, which is ridiculous because the way it was wired before you walked straight down you could turn a light on in each room, and it was done in such a good fashion. In the washroom I've got to pull a string to turn my light on. They got the stuff so mixed up.

And then he didn't put enough wattage or whatever to run the heater and air conditioner. So I had to pay another electrician to come in and fix the electricity up for the heating and air conditioning because he wouldn't do it right. Then he wouldn't put the box up. I had to pay to have two smaller boxes put up. Then they had to come down to put a regular-size box up. I gave the contractor money. He supposed to see the electricity was done. It wasn't. But I had to pay up anyway.

Vigilance, caution, and a readiness to suspect the worst would prove essential resources in this part of Gwen Rigby's journey through disaster. She concludes, as one who knows, "Tearing out the flood-damaged stuff in the house was easy; putting the house together again was a different story."

"I LOST OVER $25,000, AND IT'S STILL NOT DONE RIGHT"

The first contractor was recommended by my neighbor across the street. Once I signed a contract with him I didn't see him for months. And by the time he came, I was frustrated; I had given him $10,000. The only thing that he did was put the roof on the house. And then I found two other guys who laid the tile in my kitchen. I thought they were going to do my whole house. But they said my job wasn't big enough, and they went off somewhere else. They were looking for bigger jobs. I was like, "But you promised me. I have a whole house here. What am I supposed to do? It's not like you doing my house for free. I'm paying you." But they left anyway.

So I was in here trying to do the sheetrock by myself at that time. A friend of my sister's, he came to help. He didn't know what he was doing, and I didn't know what I was doing but we were trying to do something. My neighbor on the corner said he had a good sheetrock person. I said, "Good, send him over." He came over. I said, "Please write up a contract." After he put the sheetrock up, he wanted to charge me extra to spray a little popcorn texture on here, and I really didn't want the texture on there. And I'm still scraping off texture from my window sills and things like that. So he got the sheetrock up. But the electrician was another thing.

The electrician came to me from another neighbor. I don't know if I should tell this story. Well, I can tell this story since I'm not calling names. My neighbor brought this guy who is supposed to be an electrician by. The guy lived in Hollygrove. So I thought, "Okay, he was a neighborhood person. Alright, that's good. Patronize the neighborhood." So this guy who is supposed to be an electrician comes by and shows me his electrician license and all his paperwork. I said, "Good." Come to find out this guy was using a borrowed license. It wasn't even his. I said, "That's not what I signed up for." But that was after I had given him $4,400. He left.

I just assumed that everything worked. But I realized they didn't know what they were doing when I noticed that they had not put the light fixtures up. They were still lying on the floor. So a couple of days later I caught up to him and said, "When are you coming to put my light fixtures back up?" "Oh, we don't do that," he said. I said, "Oh hell yes, you do!" I was in the middle in the street screaming. I still have to have an electrician to come back in here to redo the bathroom because none of the lights are coming on in that room. Then the city inspector came out and inspected the electrical work. Know what? He said it was fine. What does he know? I'm still having problems with my electricity.

And the people who painted the outside of my house cost me as well. Well, by this time I was back at work and could not watch what was going on day to day. So you know what happened? These folks painted my house but did not sand it first. They painted without sanding. It's peeling now.

So I lost over $25,000, and it's still not done right. I went through four contractors and spent $25,000 more than I had to. By the time I went through my last contractor, what was left to have done? I said to myself, "Just give me a video and show me what to do and I'll do it."

In her words, "Just give me a video and show me what to do and I'll do it," Gwen Rigby captures succinctly the idea of going it alone. Not all contractors were incompetent or avaricious, but there were enough who fell into one or both categories to create significant risks for any homeowner seeking help.

Fixing up one's house was anything but a coherent, reasonable process. And while it is true that ordinary life is never as sensible as we make it out to be, it is orders of magnitude more sane than the postflood world of New Orleans. If we pay close attention to the stories found throughout this book, we begin to see that surviving the flood was only one test of human will and arguably the simpler compared to the trials that followed it. The fortuitous moments and misadventures that piled one atop the other, from evacuation to exile to the search for assistance and rebuilding remind us that it is the social and political forces set in motion by natural events that more often than not prove to be the more onerous and difficult to bear. All this would not have been lost on Freud.

WHAT FREUD COULD HAVE PREDICTED

Freud spent his career making outsize claims about the human psyche and its ill-fated bond with society. Taken together, the stories we've recounted throughout this book stand witness to one such claim: in the end, it is not our inability to control climates, predict weather, preserve our bodies from age or our minds from decay that most troubles us; what proves most intractable and perplexing in our lives are, simply put, other people. Many New Orleanians whose lives were buffeted about by Hurricane Katrina would likely find at least a jot of truth in Freud's words:

> [W]e cannot see why the regulations made by ourselves should not . . . be a protection and benefit for every one of us. And yet . . . we come upon a contention which is so astonishing that we must dwell upon it. This contention holds that what we call our civilization is largely responsible for our misery.[19]

In this last sentence is encoded the connection between the mind of Freud and the lived experience of disaster relief at a moment in history when the prevailing political-cultural ideal was one of small government and privatized public services. Hurricane Katrina and the waters she troubled damaged tens of thousands of lives. But in the end, more often of than not, these floodwaters proved markedly less worrisome than the humans who set in motion the social processes allegedly designed to repair those broken lives.[20]

As we piled interview upon interview in the course of our research it became apparent to us that for residents of Hollygrove and Pontchartrain Park, Hurricane Katrina was more than a disastrous weather event, much more. In their vivid stories, some almost elegiac, others roaring with discontent, and some told as matters of fact, it became increasingly clear that flooding itself was too limited an event to account for all—or even most—of their unforeseen and unwelcome experiences. In the telling, what we heard was one fickle experience following another like a run-on sentence with no comma or period in sight. Even those who tried to ride out the flood and ended up in harm's way found escape from danger an easier task than living in exile, applying for government assistance, and working to rebuild their houses. What can we make of this? How does the idea of disaster recovery help us to account for these experiences? How does one recover from "recovery"?

7

"THE KATRINA EFFECT"
IS THERE A CODA?

Miss Katrina is not finished with me.

JO JOHNSTON, MAY 23, 2009

The word "disaster" almost always conjures up the word "recovery." Recovery is disaster's coda. It differs in kind from evacuation, exile, seeking assistance, and rebuilding; it marks both the end of disaster and the beginning of life renewed. The Middle English prefix "re" signals a going back, as in re-turn, re-trace, re-vert—to be, in short, as we were before. Leysia Palen and her colleagues, invoking decades of research on the phases of disaster, list recovery as the last of seven stages in the human experience of catastrophe. Among the several indices of this final stage are "individual rehabilitation and readjustment [and] community restoration of property."[1] While invoking recovery might not necessarily beg that well-worn postscript "And they lived happily ever after," it nevertheless suggests a return to life rehabbed and set aright.

This, the final chapter, veers away from authority of chance to briefly examine disaster's swansong. As we write this final chapter it has been eight years since that fate-filled day in late August 2005. Most of the people we interviewed in both neighborhoods have now completed work on their houses. Most have returned to their old jobs or started new ones. They can look with some satisfaction and say, "All this I have done in the face of calamity." It might seem reasonable at this point in their journeys to understand them as recovered. Is Miss Katrina past? Is she history? Have people moved on and left her behind? Or is she more like the past that Faulkner imagined, forever haunting the present?[2]

Noah himself, our Old Testament survivor whom we first encountered in the prologue, appeared on his way to recovery in the postdeluge phase of his disaster. After the water subsided, he followed divine instructions "to build an altar to offer burnt offerings to God."[3] He started a farm. He planted a vineyard. But then, for some inexplicable reason, he began drinking heavily.[4] We might ask, Did Noah himself recover from this biblical flood? Or did this calamity continue? Did it have no ending for God's last "righteous man"? How much of the variance in Noah's long biblical life is explained by the term "disaster recovery"? And therein lay the puzzle.

We don't know how or if Noah linked his frequent use of alcohol to the frightening cataclysm he experienced. But we do know a little about how someone might look at disaster recovery from a distance and how someone who lived through disaster thinks about what it means to recover. Consider the following two quotes. The first is from John Stuart Mill, a well-known nineteenth-century philosopher. The second quote is from Cheryl Haden, a voice you have encountered at various places throughout this book. Cheryl, who lives in Pontchartrain Park, is an artist and professor of art and in her own way a philosopher. Together, Mill and Haden have something to teach us about the end of disaster.

Writing in 1848, Mill expresses his palpable faith in human nature and social institutions to rebound from the insults wrought by calamities of all kinds:

> [W]hat has so often excited wonder [is] the great rapidity with which countries recover from a state of devastation; the disappearance, in a short time, of all traces of the mischiefs done by earthquakes, floods, hurricanes, and the ravages of war. . . . [A] few years after, everything is much as it was before.[5]

Mill is writing far from disaster. He is addressing mayhem a good distance from the point of impact. Like many creative people, Professor Haden is a bit of a romantic. But her romanticism cannot erase a blunt realism born from the firsthand experience of catastrophe:

> We will forever be defined as the generation that lived through Katrina. No matter where I go for the rest of my life. When I say I'm from New Orleans, it's not Creole cooking or jazz or blues music, it's the place where Katrina happened. That's who we are. That's what we are. And so, in that respect, it'll never be in the past.

With time, disaster ends for Mill and "everything is much as it was before." For Mill, disaster has a coda. Disasters knock down; neighborhoods, towns, and cities are typically rebuilt. Disasters break up life's routines, and resilient people respond by mending the cracks and returning to some semblance of the ordinary. Recovery is a compelling final chapter in the story of wreck and ruin. "Recovery" is a word meant to signal the victory of human will and organization over destruction and misery. It is a truth, perhaps better put, a promise, that comforts. But pushing back against this final, triumphant certainty is another, found in the reflections and appraisals of those whose lives are upended by disaster. It points to where recovery's truth stops, leaving what remains unaccounted for.

If we assess Cheryl's years after the waters came, it is apparent that at least some of the mischiefs wrought by Katrina have disappeared. Cheryl's house is repaired. Her furniture is new. Her daughter is back in school and thriving. But how something looks from the outside is not necessarily how it feels on the inside. Hurricane Katrina did more than wreak havoc with the built environment and human routines. For Cheryl it seeped into her emotional and affective connection to the place she calls New Orleans. We *are* Katrina, she implies, summoning the present tense. In this way, for Cheryl, disaster continues for her and her city.

We use concepts to select from the perplexity of the social and environmental worlds we seek to know a few characteristics that we deem of sufficient importance to gather under one term and examine closely. What we sometimes fail to see is that every selection from that perplexity is also a deflection; we examine this but not that. Every concept both reveals and obscures; it points, in short, to where an explanation stops. In the discussion to follow we will point to several instances in which "disaster recovery" appears to reach the end of its tether. And we will offer up another concept to help us see how Hurricane Katrina continues in some fashion for many individuals and families in both neighborhoods.

Howard Rodin of Pontchartrain Park suggests one way in which the conventional idea of recovery might well miss some of the persistent effects of disaster:

> I guess one of the things and it still happens to me is that I still sometimes get up at four in the morning. I call that "the Katrina effect." Because many is the night while living in Baton Rouge unable to return home I would just wake up at 4 a.m. Regardless of what time I went to bed, I was wide awake at 4 a.m. I would just wake up like clockwork and stay awake. I couldn't go back to sleep. I just asked the Lord for help.

For Howard, Katrina was more than wind and water. She was an interloper who hung around long enough to reset his circadian clock. We borrow Mr. Rodin's telling expression, "the Katrina effect," to suggest that for at least some people this flood is not something they lived through but, rather, something they live with, each in his or her own way.

"I HAD A STROKE"

On a sunny Sunday morning five years after the flood, Jo Johnston walked to church. Bethany United Methodist is just a few blocks from her home in Pontchartrain Park. Sitting with friends and fellow congregants, she felt connected to what matters most in her life, her relationship with God. But Jo also felt something else that morning: "I noticed for the first time a pain on my left side. And I felt dizzy. I began to perspire." Knowing something was not right with her body, Jo left church and walked home. Her symptoms persisted and got worse. "I changed my clothes and packed a bag," she said. "I called 911 and sat myself down in the yard, waiting. An ambulance picked me up. . . . I had a stroke." Jo had a ready understanding of the origin of her medical misery. "Miss Katrina," she noted methodically, "is not finished with me."

Strokes have a complicated etiology. It is not at all certain that Jo's cerebrovascular attack is a consequence of living with the long-term uncertainty and stress that began with Hurricane Katrina. But no physician could tell her it wasn't. Her cause-and-effect way of thinking moved the disaster from past to present, making it a willful power in her life years after the flood. For her, the storm was still raging somewhere inside.

"WE MOSTLY DO FUNERALS"

But for some others, Hurricane Katrina has assumed the firmness of a conviction, as in "of course" or "it figures," independent of the data. Suggested in a recent encounter between one of the authors, Pam Jenkins, and the owner of a local flower shop is how the "facts" don't always matter when a matter-of-factness solidifies around an idea about the persistence of disaster. Pam tells this story:

> There is a small shop in Mid-City, a neighborhood roughly equal distance between Pontchartrain Park and Hollygrove. Mid-City did not escape the flooding. As the waters in the city rose to the level of the lake, Mid-City flooded with several feet in low-lying areas. Among the hundreds of once waterlogged structures in this faubourg sits the flower shop, just a few steps away from the trolley line. An unpretentious store, it takes up a little more or less than 1,000 square feet.
>
> I trade here, buying fresh-cut flowers and plants. One day, more than four years after the flood, I had an occasion to ask the owner that by-now common Katrina question "How's business since the storm?" His first answer was rote. "Fine," he said briskly. He paused at that point, perhaps

rethinking "fine" and began to talk thoughtfully about the changes in his business. He was still busy, he said, waving his hand about the shop cluttered with fresh flowers, plants, and half-done orders. But business had changed since the flood. Before the storm, customers bought flowers for a wide range of events, including weddings, anniversaries, and birthdays. But since the hurricane and flood, he said, looking away, "We mostly do funerals."

His business is "fine" post-Katrina, but the market for flowers has shifted to commemorating life's final passage. Implied here and what many people in the city believe is that after Katrina the rate of mortality increased. And yet, belying the link between an increase in funeral flowers and deaths in New Orleans is the simple fact that the city's mortality rate did not go up noticeably following the retreat of the waters.[6] And while violent crime in the city remains well above the national average, it is not markedly higher since 2005.[7] But statistics and perception are not always synchronized. The point is there is a belief, widely shared among city residents rich and poor, that the awful power of Katrina continues to haunt the course of life's twists and turns. Beliefs, we know, can be more irresistible than facts.

Perhaps not surprisingly, while the rate of mortality in the city did not increase following the flood, the etiology of death post-Katrina did change somewhat, in part, as Jo Johnston's stroke would seem to suggest, due to the stresses of recovery itself. In *Markets of Sorrow*, Vincanne Adams recounts the story of a widow who lost her husband to a stroke shortly after their return to a rehabbed house in Gentilly, a neighborhood next to Pontchartrain Park. The couple struggled unsuccessfully for years to access Road Home funds that were dedicated to help people like them. In the end, their house was rebuilt by an army of volunteers. For the widow, it was the callous and disorganized Road Home program that killed her husband. In her words: "(I)t wasn't Hurricane Katrina that killed him. It was the recovery that killed him . . . Look what they did to him."[8]

"I GUESS YOU COULD SAY I RECOVERED"

Also worth noting is the way someone who has lived through disaster and so much more speaks about recovery. The colloquial use of the word "recovery" may disguise the lived experiences of trauma.

In the spring of 2009 we spoke with Jesse Gray about life after Katrina. He and his wife, Diane, were once again living in Hollygrove. Their house had been rehabbed, their yard was trimmed and neat, and Jesse's famed truck with close to 300,000 miles looked like he had just driven it out of the showroom. This resilient couple would seem to typify the ideal of disaster recovery.

In the course of our conversation we asked Jesse about himself. How was he doing not quite four years after the flood? He replied,

> About a year ago I started having nightmares. I take pills for nightmares . . . anxiety. I couldn't get rid of my nightmares. I'd wake up at night soaking wet. I'd be depressed all the time. They're rough, man. I know it's a nightmare. I've been trying to wake up right, but you can't wake up right.

We also asked Jesse about the neighborhood. Had it recovered? His response was both clever and, unbeknown to us or him, a portent. "I guess we've recovered," he said dryly. "Crime is back; police sirens are blaring." Just over a year later we spoke with Jesse again. His post-Katrina nightmares continued but now were filled with shadows from a tragedy no parent should endure.

On May 19, 2010, in the antiseptic prose common to police-blotter news, the following account appeared:

> Officials have identified a man killed Wednesday in a Mid-City shooting as Lester J. [Gray] of New Orleans, 21. [He] died of a single gunshot wound to the head.[9]

We interviewed Jesse again that summer. While he continued to employ the term "recovery," it is now meant to sum up his efforts to stay reasonably sane in a world, by all accounts, bent on testing his sanity:

> Since Katrina and, you know, then my son got killed, I've been taking time to see a psychiatrist once a month. And I go to a PTSD group twice a month. And I got all my teeth pulled out of my mouth. And I sing in the choir on weekends. I guess you could say that I recovered.

We might imagine Jesse completing a post-Katrina survey that asked whether he would identify himself as someone who has recovered. He would likely have answered, "Yes, I guess you could say so," or something to that effect. But a closer look at his life experiences during and after this historic flood suggest otherwise. It is worth noting that Jesse not only lost his son to a violent crime; he also lost his brother and his mother a few years after the waters had retreated. Whatever recovery might be, it is arguably not seeing a psychiatrist once a month and attending a PTSD group twice a month five years after a disaster.

Jesse's story is one reason we should question the matter-of-fact predictability of disaster recovery. But his story points to more than the ways "recovery" can become a gloss obscuring a complexity not typically considered when we ponder the end of disaster. The fact is, Jesse did not face Hurricane Katrina and the misshapen efforts at disaster assistance removed from life's other mundane and sometimes tragic troubles. No one does. He had to steer his way through disaster buffeted by the cruelest of fates. By following his journey from the flooding of New Orleans in 2005, to evacuating and living in exile, to returning and rebuilding, to losing his son to murder in 2010, to a year later finding Jesse on his porch and sitting down for one last chat, we've had occasion to watch and listen as one person weathered the mayhem of an unforgettable flood and all that followed it only to face a parent's true nightmare. How much of the trajectory in Jesse's experience is explained by the word "recovery"?

Like Jesse, Gwen Rigby could not talk about recovery without tying it to other events that challenged her to summon the personal strength to slog on. Not quite a year after the hurricane, Gwen was called to the hospital because her grandmother was dying, and more death followed:

> And then two days after we buried my grandmother, my niece was killed in an automobile accident on the way back to South Carolina coming from a funeral. I still haven't grieved yet, but eventually it will come out. I don't know when, but it will come because my sister has since had a nervous breakdown, and I had to go to Houston and take care of her and get her situated in the hospital.

Gwen reminds us that while the personal experiences of disaster might well encourage someone to indulge her feelings, her life is attached to others who are themselves struggling to find a way. Sometimes recovery from disaster must find a place in life's queue, somewhere between one heartache and another.

Our lives are spent in the present, responding to the past and anticipating the future. How catastrophe sits on this continuum is likely to be singularly personal, as is each of our lives. If we acknowledge the human continuum, how do we parse the idea of the human experience of disaster recovery? The question itself draws attention to the limiting effects of language in our efforts to represent the ways fate may well pile one blow upon another, blurring the lines of disaster, disease, death, and so on.

We've offered several accounts thus far; each is an appeal to see the limitations of this master concept in accounting for the long-term effects of catastrophe on the body and mind. Although different one from the other, what they share is a focus on the interior of the person: on a circadian rhythm, on a cerebrovascular rupture, on a mode of reasoning, on a psychic trauma. But the stories people told us of "recovery" further complicate the term. Some people helped us see the tie between life after impact and the personal observations and appraisals they made of their neighborhoods. If disaster, by definition, disrupts the relationships we have with our built and modified environments, coming to terms with life after disaster will be connected in some fashion to our interpretations of the kinds and qualities of those places months and years later.[10] One might well estimate how much he has recovered by paying attention to the streets, the houses, and the people that make up his neighborhood postdisaster.

THE PERSONAL-COLLECTIVE NEXUS IN HOLLYGROVE

Between 2000 and 2010 New Orleans lost over 140,000 residents. It also became wealthier and whiter. While the city's median household income increased by almost 40 percent in a decade, the increase in median household income in Hollygrove from 2000 to 2010 was about half that rate; and the poverty rate remained steady at the city average of 27 percent. Hollygrove was not a particularly resilient neighborhood before the flood. It was less so after.

Jerry Wright graduated high school in 2009. He grew up amid the temptations available in a troubled urban environment:

> Yeah, a lot of people I went to school with before the storm, they didn't go to school after that. . . . [T]his dude who stays right across the street from me, I've been friends with him all my life, stopped going to school, started selling drugs and stuff. Now I really hang with my family. I do everything with my family members so it doesn't really bother me. I don't be outside like that to get in trouble or get caught up in nothing.

Nights can be especially troubling in Hollygrove. Bo Gray saw that trouble in the eyes of many young people he had known since they were babies but no longer recognizes in the tumultuous years after Katrina:

> The young people in your neighborhood, they crazy . . . Stay away from them. There ain't nothing for the kids to do back here. Nowhere to go, you know; they like hanging 'round, and you know, you can't tell them nothing, you know. You know, you got to get out of their way.

Jerry and Bo are generations apart in age. Yet each looks at the streets of Hollygrove and sees remnants of Katrina in the lives of young people about

7.1. Two abandoned houses in Hollygrove in 2011, six years after the flood.
Photo by Mary Byers Truslow.

them who—vulnerable before the flood—are noticeably more volatile and risk-prone years after the water retreated.

Difficult times for some children in Hollygrove extend to not having enough food to eat and having an understandable sense of desperation to escape the drugs and violence, both inside and outside their homes. Jean Stetson, a local pastor, cannot disconnect her personal path away from Katrina from her experiences with scared and hungry children:

> I was over here [at church] one day 'cause a store had given me a pallet of candy like sometimes they do . . . you know, the Easter candy or Halloween candy. Well I started calling some of the little kids in from the neighborhood. And one of them, his name was Joe, and he might have been nine or ten years old or something like that. I said, "Hey honey, look what I got. I got some candy." Well I was in the dining room, you know, and my cook was fixing these plates to send out. I said, "Here, I've got some candy for you." He took a look at the candy and looked at the food. And remember, this is broccoli, turkey, and rice. Looked at the candy and looked at the food and started handing the candy back. He said, "Mama Jean, can I have some food?" I lost it!

In these brief vignettes Jerry, Bo, and Jean remind us that recovery from disaster is never simply an inner-directed accomplishment. It is also connected to the sense we make of the lives and habitats of those others who are part of life in our communities and neighborhoods. The "I" in our personal recovery, in other words, is connected, in part, to the "we" in our collective life.

THE PERSONAL-COLLECTIVE NEXUS
IN PONTCHARTRAIN PARK

A more visible demonstration of the tie between personal recovery and the perceived quality of neighborhood life is found in Pontchartrain Park. It is in this historic neighborhood where demographic change is most evident, starting with a 43 percent decline in population between 2000 and 2010. In recent decades, as children moved out, the population of the neighborhood aged. Thirty percent were over sixty-five in 2005, the year of the flood. The flood accelerated population decline as many seniors sold their homes and moved to other neighborhoods and cities. The proportion over sixty-five in 2010 dropped to 21.6 percent, and the proportion of renters tripled, many of them single parents with kids. In the process, median household income in Pontchartrain Park declined by more than 13 percent in ten years as the proportion of residents living in poverty more than doubled (table 7.1).

For David Sawyer and his wife, Katherine, in their late thirties, their neighborhood is simply not the same place since the flood. David and Katherine returned to Pontchartrain Park determined to remake their lives. Their plan was to rebuild a once-proud house soaked to the bones by two weeks of standing water several feet deep. This ratty, stressful task they accomplished with both of them working full-time jobs. Five years after the disaster, they had a new plan. Although David was born and raised in Pontchartrain Park and baptized in St. Gabriel's Catholic Church just a few streets away, they've decided to move elsewhere, as David explains.

"WE FEEL LIKE WE'RE IN A STRANGE TOWN"

The golf course is still in rough shape. I used to take my walks there. Sometimes I would fish in the little pond for bass and perch. These were nice little outings, like therapy for me. I can't do that anymore. The houses in the neighborhood, many of them, are still boarded up. More and more I see people in the neighborhood I don't even know, that I've never seen before, strangers. . . .

TABLE 7.1. Demographic changes in Hollygrove, Pontchartrain Park, and New Orleans, 2000–2010

Area	Hollygrove		Pontchartrain Park		New Orleans	
Year	2000	2010	2000	2010	2000	2010
Total population	6,919	4,377	2,630	1,482	484,674	343,829
Proportion black	0.947	0.941	0.970	0.974	0.666	0.597
Median household income	$30,659	$36,819	$44,070	$38,073	$43,176	$59,952
Proportion living in poverty	0.284	0.267	0.102	0.260	0.279	0.270
Proportion owner-occupied	0.542	0.506	0.921	0.797	0.465	0.480
Proportion renters	0.458	0.494	0.070	0.203	0.535	0.520
Proportion children <18 years	0.270	0.255	0.206	0.246	0.267	0.210
Proportion over age 65	0.155	0.163	0.316	0.216	0.117	0.109
Proportion female householder w/children	0.224	0.216	0.115	0.191	0.177	0.137
Median house value	$65,900	$127,300	$73,700	$131,000	$87,300	$184,100

Sources: Data from Greater New Orleans Community Data Center, 2011, "Neighborhood Statistical Areas: Statistical Profiles," www.gnocdc.org (accessed December 2011); and New Orleans, Louisiana, at American Fact Finder, U.S. Census Bureau, http://factfinder2.census.gov/faces/nav/jsf/pages/community_facts.xhtml (accessed November 2014).

We had this woman from the projects that moved in down the street. She played her music twenty-four/seven on full blast. I called the police on her. It stopped. Next thing you know, people are breaking into houses. They broke into our house. Before Katrina we knew almost everybody who lived here. Yeah, you know, if you saw a bum on the street, you knew the bum. You knew who a person was, where he lived, who he lived with. Not anymore. Strangers walk the streets. We feel like we're in a strange town.

What David and Katherine experienced face to face literally and figuratively are the demographic changes that followed the flooding of Pontchartrain Park. They could not help but notice that their patch of the world had not recovered, if by "recovery" is meant a return of the old, familiar faces and neighborhood routines; it had, rather, become unfamiliar territory. In a word, they felt estranged from what had once been home. For them, Katrina was not past; she was all too present in strange faces, in acts of vandalism, in the loss of a boyhood place that served as a retreat from the daily grind.

Alayna, who lives a few streets away from the Sawyers, has a hard time with the idea of recovery. She looks about her neighborhood and sees more entropy than order and wonders aloud at how little is known, some forty-eight months after the storm, about who, what, where, and how to restore that order.

"I DON'T THINK THAT'S RECOVERY, DO YOU?"

It is more than four years since the hurricane and . . . there are homes with overgrown grass because nobody takes responsibility for it. They don't know where the homeowner is, or the homeowner doesn't know how to navigate this maze. They don't know who to go to or how to work with them once they get there. You know, even for an educated person, it's a maze to get through, and there aren't any instructions. Or I haven't seen any. The city can't even keep the grass cut on these vacant properties. I don't think that's recovery, do you? I don't think we've recovered.

A wise saying heard now and then resonates a bit with David's and Alayna's appraisals of Pontchartrain Park: "We don't see things as they are; we see things as we are."[11] Suggested here is the idea that recovery is, at least in part, in the seeing, in this case in the seeing of the neighborhood as something other and uncomfortably different.[12]

7.2. A property in Pontchartrain Park in 2010, five years after the flood.
Photo by Skip Bolen.

AND FINALLY, FROM HOME TO HOUSE

The idea of a stubborn strangeness born with disaster and not fading away with the passage of time also can be connected to the homestead, the house itself. Pamela Harold had lived in her Hollygrove home for almost five decades prior to the flood. She is now back in her remade house, but going on four years after the flood it was no longer a home, a place that comforts.

Everybody comes in here saying, "I don't know what you're talking about, this house looks nice and what-not." To me it doesn't feel nice. I mean, I didn't joyfully move out, get my house fixed up, and move back here. What I did, we all did, was painful; it was laborious; it was hard. I look at a corner and think I see a piece of furniture that I used to love. But it's not there. A picture used to hang here and over there. Why aren't they there now? There's so many different fibers in a home. It's not just a house, it is layers of things and memories.

These many and varied passages from residents of the two neighborhoods underline the complexity of what we are calling, borrowing from Howard Rodin, "the Katrina effect."

Reclaiming what disaster takes from a person—sleep, health, a sense of well-being, neighborhood, a place called home, and so on—is most likely not a process with a definitive endpoint. Repairing a house, putting a neighborhood back on the power grid, reopening shuttered businesses, sponsoring a music festival are different sorts of achievements than restoring that unique sense of personhood that shaped life before disaster strikes. Is it likely that a person who lived through this historic flood will gather up the loose ends of her life, tie them together as they once were, and proceed down the road, recovered? Do such existential triumphs occur? Or are we asking the wrong question?

RECOVERY OR EDITING?

Disaster recovery is an abstraction that cannot carry the weight of the stories we have presented in this final chapter and throughout the book. If no disaster begins at impact—a lesson learned from the good work of anthropologists—it is probably also true that no disaster ends by invoking the word "recovered."[13] The Katrina effect continues in one way or another for the many people we interviewed. There is an inevitable contrast between the one-of-a-kind-ness of a human life and the poverty of the principles we devise to understand that life. Hence we are by no means making a case for killing off this foundational concept. Concepts and measures that track the mending and improvement of towns and cities and the people who inhabit them are necessary.

Our quarrel with the abstraction "recovery" is its seductive power to stop inquiry in its tracks. It has about it the quality of a final vocabulary.[14] Once we invoke it we can stop the conversation and turn our attention to the next calamity. Our counsel is to use it while at the same time looking to see where it does not apply, where people, lives, and places are something other than recovered. The questions "What do people do in the face of overwhelming calamity?" and "How do they slog on amidst total ruin, or do they?" will continue to invite our attention, while our various answers to these queries will, by necessity, be temporary.

What we found in a close-up look at the lives of people in two neighborhoods devastated by disaster reminds us more of editing than of recovery. As we write, Cheryl, Howard, Jesse, Jo, Pamela, Alayna, David, and Katherine, and the many others who were kind enough to speak with us are amending and revising their lives, cutting here, splicing there, adding and deleting, all in some way self-consciously responding to this historic flood.

The shock the water delivered continues in the day-to-day ways people think about New Orleans, experience themselves and their bodies, make mundane sense of the way the world works, join groups, make decisions, and so on.

"Editing" is an abstraction, too; but this one simply comes closer to what we heard and saw over the years we spent talking with people and walking the neighborhoods. We are not invoking it to bring discussion to a close; it is after all a temporary answer to a perennial question. It is offered in the spirit of "Have a look. Does the idea of editing help you spot something that invites further inquiry?"[15] For us, it throws a bit of light on how people altered their lives to create a better fit between themselves and the changes Hurricane Katrina put in motion. What the dozens of people who gave their time and thought to this project taught us is that the best one can do is learn to adapt to the changes wrought by disaster, cobbling the lessons learned into an intelligible life.

Writing in 2009, Natasha Trethewey describes her brother's travails four years after the Gulf Coast was struck by the blunt force of Hurricane Katrina. In her thought-filled prose she writes,

> I learn more about the difficulties he faces every day. I see in his contemplation the incorporation of a new narrative, one that integrates his past with the uncertain future he faces.[16]

In a more prosaic but no less convincing style, Marie Saunders, a longtime resident of Hollygrove, connects the idea of editing to spoken words, ending her brief account of her son's life after Katrina with a prescient observation on the need to tell about disaster:

> I have a son that's going through some stuff after this flood. . . . He survived the storm . . . He was able to get to Tulane, and there was some people there and they were able to get a boat or something. And he was able to get to Texas. He's on the streets now. He gets an apartment and he can't hold it. But yet I'm told that he is okay if he stays on his medicine. But if you are mentally ill, how are you going to do that? So it was tough before the hurricane, and it's even tougher now. But if we are going to survive this or anything else, stories are all we have. We have to talk about it. We can't sit around and be quiet. That doesn't get us anywhere.

Editing life after disaster is as varied as the people whose lives beg some annotating and rearranging. Denise Anders is reassembling herself this way:

In the end it comes down to this: just preparing yourself to be able to take care of yourself without relying on someone else. I guess it made me stronger . . . and more of a fighter as I go on. . . . We'll see.

Michael Carrington is amending his life by becoming more introspective:

I think I try to reason, analyze my way out of it, and in some ways denied that there were a lot of feelings going on and tried to repress those. That still, I think, impacts me even four years later. Because I thought I could get over it without actually going through the feelings that are natural to go through . . . I still have to work on this.

Tori Clarksdale has lost part of her history, sending her on a journey to connect a missing past with a present and a future:

I lost pictures of my grandmother who is dead and my uncle that has passed, 'cause it's like your whole past is wiped away, you know, you don't have pictures, you don't have proof. Stuff you did have proof about is gone. So, it's really like you never existed, like that person never was real, you know. That's the part that really makes me sad. It's like they died again . . . me, I've got to go on.

Bo, Jesse's brother, died of complications from cancer and heart disease in 2008. We spoke with Bo two months before his death. In his closing chapter, he was busy editing what was left of his life, narrating a story of lost freedom and the felt need to keep on keeping on:

You know, it's really not the same. I didn't say it was no worse, but it's not the same as it was. Back then I think I had more freedom. Now, I think I might have gotten tied down. You got so many new things on your mind. Like I say, it ain't the same. You be trying, you trying to make things, you know, be as they was; but it's really not like it was, you know. So, you got to keep going.

"Disaster management," viewed from the vantage point of its most elemental unit, the individual, is perhaps nothing more or less than the stories people tell over time about how and what they did to survive, to get through, to live another day. If we are going to survive this or anything else, Marie Saunders suggests, "stories are all we have." What if at this most personal level the management of catastrophe is in the telling and the retelling? Perhaps we manage bedlam, creating some semblance of control, by editing our lives in and after disaster in order to give a more or less coherent account of what otherwise likely appears as unintelligible.

A fitting way to conclude this discussion is to call once again on one of the voices who spoke our story into existence. In Jo Johnston's words,

> And, with Miss Katrina, that's where you leave it. You take one day at a time, and you learn to do what must be done. Maybe you were doing it before, but you do it with grace now. . . . And you talk about it.

IS THIS "GOODBYE" KATRINA?

The World Meteorological Organization (WMO) retired "Katrina" in recognition of the carnage and ruin she precipitated. Chris Vaccaro, a spokesman with the National Oceanic and Atmospheric Administration, explains: "When a storm causes widespread destruction or loss of life, its name is retired, not only to avoid reminding the victims of the horrors they experienced but also to keep the record straight."[17] It is far easier, of course, for the WMO to retire the name of a hurricane than it is for those whose lives it altered to forget and return to what was.

EPILOGUE
MAKING A SPACE FOR CHANCE

Above all, one should not wish to divest
existence of its rich ambiguity.

FRIEDRICH NIETZSCHE, *THE GAY SCIENCE*

Over the past several years we listened to people in Pontchartrain Park and Hollygrove who talked to us about the flood, evacuating, living in exile, laboring to access disaster assistance, and rebuilding in a broken city.[1] What caught our attention early on were the marked differences in the stories we were told; each person made his or her unique way through the hall of mirrors that was Hurricane Katrina and all that followed. What happens when uncertainty blows with a gale force that makes one's life a proverbial house of cards, when life is lived on a hunch or a guess? But it was not what the unforeseen did to each of the people who spoke with us that mattered most; it was, rather, how each of them navigated a life lived while skidding sideways.

How do people think and act in a protracted catastrophic moment when the odds against succeeding in this or that task seem, at times, insurmountable? If by the word "people" we have in mind working-class people and middle-class people, we did find some differences in the experiences and responses to chance between people in Pontchartrain Park and in Hollygrove.

Relative material advantage did shape some experiences, softening the hard edges of crazy for those who happened to have more "cheese." The class distinction promised a familiar story, one of sufficient order to allow prediction, the master narrative of our craft. But the patterns and trajectories of the lives we encountered in each neighborhood were anything but foreclosed, as comforting as this idea might be to some psychologists and sociologists. As their varied experiences with the ill-managed Road Home Program illustrate, with or without "cheese," chance and its cognates were in charge. Predictability and its familiars, foreseeable and reliable, arrived late on the scene, if they showed up at all.

We knew from our own work in this field that vast tracks of lives lived in disaster are likely to be overlooked by our most approved social and psychological authorities. Those of us who study people and society are taught to embrace the rational turn, to search out the orderly arrangement of things, to ignore as inconsequential the quirky and coincidental.

We are alarmed by the possibility of the causeless. We crave that which produces effects, sequences, series, chains. Our habit is to skate over happenstance to get to the next orderly arrangement. Accidental appearances are just that, accidental, and can either be dispensed with or redefined in such a manner as to make them a part of a class or system.

Worthy social inquiry, in short, is dedicated to rescuing the determined from the contingent, to borrowing or coining abstractions that would identify continuities or overarching conditions of probability; the accidental may well occur but need not be brought to analytic attention. With a bit of searching, however, we found some credible allies in our efforts to free chance and its confederates from the determined, to carve out a place for the unforeseen in the study of disaster.

Annoyed by the work of the social Darwinists who reduced the complexity of psychology and sociology to a few simple biological axioms, William James pointed to the bias in the logic of the concept or abstraction that promised a step forward in the academic mastery of human nature. For him, constructs and classifications are meant to sweep the untidiness of quotidian experiences into a pile, one sufficiently coherent to bear the weight of a word or two. Writing more than century ago, James purposely dodged the tidiness of the orderly to throw some light on providence, chance, and serendipity; these were for him among life's first principles. "Restore the vague," he once commanded, "to its rights."[2]

More than six decades after James advocated for an indeterminism that placed the fuzzy and imprecise square within the study of psychology, Dennis Wrong warned sociologists away from an "oversocialized" view of the person and "an overintegrated view of society."[3] Both the person and society, he reasons, are not as norm-driven and social as we are taught to imagine. Two decades later, Charles Perrow issued a heretical call to those who study society, one James and Wrong would have found agreeable. The idea of social order, he notes, is a powerful trope that might well blind us to the raw quirkiness and unpredictability of human life. Perrow encourages those of us who study the social to write the disorder and randomness of everyday life into our articles and books. His words are meant to provoke:

I can only plead that [the] nonrational, changeable, multifaceted . . . be put back at the center of the social sciences, so that scholars can better tolerate the disorder, even appreciate its virtues. . . . [M]uch of what happens is the result of happenstance, accidents, misunderstandings, and random . . . behavior.[4]

Perrow warned those of us who study society to avoid the hubris of claiming to have discovered underlying orders and systems that account for the variance in human lives. At street level, in situ, he reasoned, life is less systemic and predictable and more contradictory, and disordered. Who we are, where we are, and what we are doing today, he cautioned, cannot be readily explained by social structures or forces that fashion for each of us a destiny; personal life is too untidy and chaotic for that. Classifying and ordering can do little more than imprison the uncertainty of human life in a prepared vocabulary, as if to tame chance itself.

In their pleas to place the messiness of lived experience square within the purview of the psychologist and sociologist, James, Wrong, and Perrow called attention to the inescapable randomness of the everyday. Their words breathe life into the moribund language of a sociology desperate to bring some order to disorder, as if chaos itself could be written out of the literature by not letting it in. What we sociologists call "society," in short, is more often than we care to admit the product of historical accidents.

And yet, anyone—even those of us who call the academy home—knows at some visceral level that the structure of our lives is neither fixed nor all that foreseeable. Our individual lives are subject to the whims of fortune and misfortune even when the outcome for a group or class to which we belong can be statistically predicted. We humans are, as James notes, "in great measure in the hands of chance."[5]

But while we do know deep in our own skins that life is never as ordered as the purveyors of systems and organizations would have us believe, we also know that ordinary life is not without a discernible scheme, a more or less predictable format that directs our attention to this or that, guides our behaviors, and informs our feelings. Order—or at least the one we imagine—leads bafflement in a choreographed gavotte that we know as the ordinary.

Disaster disorders this dance. Larger than life, bafflement now leads, often seeming to take the floor alone, as if order has left the dance. Hurricane Katrina created what we might call a post-positivist world, one rife with problems that defy solutions. In this alternate universe people become subject to forces that exceed life's normal strategies for making sense and getting on day to day. It is worth remembering that the prefix "dis" in disaster comes from the Greek "dus," or "bad." We join "dis" to "order" when we want to signal a breakdown or collapse of organization and regulation. "Aster," by the way, is Greek for "star." Disaster—literally "bad star," celestial mayhem—invokes those sudden moments when confusion is in charge, and we are left wondering what will become of us.

We purposely did not seek to explain Miss Katrina; our goal, rather, was to make a piece of her world a bit more complex, to create a little muddle of our own. Amending a line from Terry Eagleton, we intended to wreak a bit of mayhem on the customary language of social studies in order to knock loose a few insights that as a matter of course go unnoticed in the study of disaster.[6] After all, if subatomic physics can add chance to cause and effect, surely a few of us sociologists can do the same.

Perhaps the most visible example of this disorderly conduct is in the final chapter, where we mount a challenge to the hegemony of the master trope "disaster recovery." If the idea of recovery haunted the margins of this book, a second concept was close at hand, begging a mention. Let's examine for a moment that now stylish term "resilience." It is hard to read a contemporary sociological account of disaster that does not include this concept.

Building resilience, social capital and resilience, partnerships for disaster resilience—the topics are many and varied.[7] But the seductive appeal of this concept puts some distance between those who live through disasters and those of us who want to understand what that experience is like. One recent and well-regarded book on the topic defines resilience as "the ability to prepare and plan for, absorb, recover from, and more successfully adapt to adverse events."[8] How, we might ask, does this abstraction help us understand the many and varied stories recounted in this book?

To shed a bit of light on this question, let's leave this disaster for a moment and travel back in time to a small town in northeastern Pennsylvania and another kind of mayhem. From the early 1980s on, Centralia gained nationwide attention as the ill-fated village sitting atop an underground mine fire. Among the random notes Kroll-Smith and Couch jotted down while living in Centralia, studying the personal and social responses to the fire, is this one:

> At a meeting of the Centralia Borough Council Mary H. asked this question: "Why is it taking so long to get those gas monitors in our houses? We go to bed afraid each night." "We're working on that," was the quick reply from a Department of Mines official. At his response, Mary simply cried. She sobbed. We could hear it in the back of the room. Talk stopped.

Mary cried. Clearing his throat, the DOM official promised to check on the status of the monitoring equipment and get back to Mary in the next day or two. He did.[9]

Mary cried publicly, the world moved a bit in response, she soon got a carbon monoxide monitor in her house, as did many of her neighbors. In her moment of overt emotion, was Mary "successfully adapting to" an adverse event? Did she "prepare" and "plan ahead" to ask a question, cry, and get what she desired in response? Was Mary resilient, refusing to "absorb" the official's response? Or does this abstraction miss what is unique about a woman who, when faced with a curt, dismissive response from a public official, found her voice in tears, a cry that arguably altered, if only faintly, the course of official response to a potentially lethal gas?[10] These rhetorical questions are the types of queries that bedevil our field; they will be read with a bit of a smile by those who struggle with them.

If it is not contingency in disaster that matters most but what people do moment by moment when faced with it, how might their thoughts, feelings, and actions complicate the definitive notion of resilience? Planning for resilience in the face of disaster does make some sense. But acknowledging that plans, policies, and procedures are more like those proverbial wishes that go unanswered than blueprints for the human response to havoc begs the next question: Just what do people do when faced with the madness of disaster impact?

The maelstrom that was and continues in many ways to be Hurricane Katrina has much to teach us about how people feel, think, and act when faced with the unforeseen and the contingent. To believe that what is social is ultimately orderly—as illusory as that is—seems to be essential for getting on in the world as disaster managers, as sociologists and, perhaps, as survivors of disaster.[11] Among her many lessons, Miss Katrina taught us something about how to think and write about disorder, less to make it orderly, and more to remind us that the world is irreducibly chancy.

NOTES

FOREWORD BY ELIJAH ANDERSON

1. Solomon Northup, 1853, *Twelve Years a Slave: Narrative of Solomon Northup, a Citizen of New-York, Kidnapped in Washington City in 1841, and Rescued in 1853* (Auburn, NY: Derby and Miller), 82.

2. W.E.B. Du Bois, 1994 [1903], *The Souls of Black Folk* (New York: Dover), 9.

3. For a fuller account of the intersection of race, slavery, and deindustrialization, see Elijah Anderson, 2006, "Inadequate Reponses, Limited Expectations," in *Rebuilding Urban Places after Disaster: Lessons from Hurricane Katrina*, edited by Eugenie L. Birch and Susan M. Wachter, 193–200 (Philadelphia: University of Pennsylvania Press).

PROLOGUE

1. Charles Perrow, 1982, "Disintegrating Social Sciences," *Phi Delta Kappan* 63(10): 686.

2. Arnold Fruchtenbaum, 2009, *The Book of Genesis* (San Antonio: Ariel Ministries Press), 14–22.

3. Bill Faulkner, 2001, "Towards a Framework for Disaster Management," *Tourism Management* 2:135–147; Brent W. Ritchie, 2004, "Chaos, Crises, and Disasters: A Strategic Approach to Crisis Management in the Tourism Industry," *Tourism Management* 25:669–683; Christine Pearson and Ian Mitroff, 1993, "From Crisis Prone to Crisis Prepared: A Framework for Crisis Management," *Academy of Management Executives* 7(1): 48–59.

4. Kenneth Hewitt, 1983, "The Idea of Calamity in a Technocratic Age," in *Interpretation of Calamity: From the Viewpoint of Human Ecology*, edited by Kenneth Hewitt (Boston: Allen), 10.

5. We borrowed the metaphor of the map from Michael Perelman, 2006, *Railroading Economics* (New York: Monthly Review Press), 21–22.

6. William James, 1897/1956, *The Will to Believe and Other Essays in Popular Philosophy* (reprint, New York: Dover), 47.

INTRODUCTION: WATER, CONVERSATIONS, AND RACE

1. The epigraph is from Jonathan Edwards, 1754/1908, *Careful Enquiry into the Freedom of Will* (reprint, Princeton, NJ: Presbyterian Board of Publication and Sabbath School Work), 20.

2. Lawrence N. Powell, 2013, *The Accidental City: Improvising New Orleans* (Cambridge: Harvard University Press), 42.

3. Ibid., 49–51.

4. Powell, 2013.

5. Richard Campanella, 2007, "Above-Sea-Level New Orleans: The Residential Capacity of Orleans Parish's Higher Ground," Center for Bioenvironmental Research, April, http://richcampanella.com/assets/pdf/study_Campanella%20analysis %20on%20Above-Sea-Level%20New%20Orleans.pdf (accessed August 2008).

6. Deon Roberts, 2008, "Drainage Veteran Calls for Greater Pump Capacity," *New Orleans City Business*, June 3; see also Earthea Nance, 2009, "Responding to Risk: The Making of Hazard Mitigation Strategy in Post-Katrina New Orleans," *Journal of Contemporary Water Research and Education* 141 (March): 21–30.

7. Independent Levee Investigation Team, 2006, "History of the New Orleans Flood Protection System," http://www.ce.berkeley.edu/projects/neworleans/report /CH_4.pdf (accessed April 2007).

8. R. B. Seed et al., 2006, *Investigation of the Performance of the New Orleans Flood Protection Systems*, report to National Science Foundation, July 31, chapter 4, "History of the New Orleans Flood Protection System," http://digitalcommons .calpoly.edu/cgi/viewcontent.cgi?article=1032&context=cenv_fac (accessed August 2010).

9. *NOVA*, 2005, "Storm that Drowned a City," November, http://www.pbs.org /wgbh/nova/orleans/struggle.html; see also Todd Shallat, 2000, "In the Wake of Hurricane Betsy," in *Transforming New Orleans and Its Environs*, edited by Craig E. Colton (Pittsburgh, University of Pittsburgh Press), 121–137.

10. Frances Frank Marcus, 1995, "Violent Storm Inundates New Orleans," *New York Times*, May 10.

11. The human propensity to personify dramatic dangers, particularly those found somewhere in nature, is nicely illustrated in a brief essay William James wrote about his personal experience of the 1906 San Francisco earthquake and fire:

I personified the earthquake as a permanent individual entity. It was *the* earthquake . . . which had been lying low and holding itself back during all the intervening months, in order, on that lustrous April morning, to invade my room. . . . It came, moreover, directly to *me*. It stole in behind my back, and once inside the room, had me all to itself, and could manifest itself convincingly. Animus and intent were never more present in any human action, nor did any human activity ever more definitely point back to a living agent as its source and origin. All whom I consulted on the point agreed as to this feature in their experience. "It expressed intention," "It was vicious," "It was bent on destruction," "It wanted to show its power," or what not. To me, it wanted simply to manifest the full meaning of its name. But what was this "It"? To some, apparently, a vague demonic power; to me an individualized being.

William James, 1911, *On Memories and Studies* (London: Longman's Green), 207–210.

12. Jere Longman and Maria Newman, 2005, "Water Pours over Levee, Flooding Dozens of Blocks in New Orleans," *New York Times*, September 23.

13. Among our mentors in this art of conversation is Studs Terkel, who notes,

> There are questions, of course. But they were casual in nature . . . the kind you would ask while having a drink with someone; the kind he would ask you. . . . In short, it was a conversation. In time, the sluice gates of damned up hurts and dreams were open.

Another is Hannah Arendt, who, in thinking of the Holocaust, draws on different words to describe the significance of conversation in creating some narrative order around the welter of human pain: "The impact of factual reality, like all other human experiences, needs speech if it is to survive the moment of experience, needs talk and communication with others to remain sure of itself." Studs Terkel, 1972, *Working* (New York: Avon), xxv; Hannah Arendt, 1968, introduction to *Illuminations*, by Walter Benjamin (New York: Harcourt Brace), 25.

14. Eric Hobsbawm, 1994, *The Age of Extremes* (New York: Vintage Books), 52.

15. That lively expression is found in William James, 1890/1950, *Principles of Psychology* (reprint, Mineola, NY: Dover Press), 2:462.

16. Howard Becker addresses the audience question this way: "[S]ome works about society present themselves, we could say, 'to whom it may concern': to any competent member of the society who might be interested"; Becker, 2007, *Telling about Society* (Chicago: University of Chicago Press, 2007), 64.

17. Clifford Geertz, 2000, *Available Light, Anthropological Reflections on Philosophical Topics* (Princeton, NJ: Princeton University Press), xi.

18. Clifford Geertz, 1988, *Works and Lives* (Stanford CA: Stanford University Press), 16.

19. In their evocative essay "Why Anthropologists Study Disaster," Anthony Oliver-Smith and Susanna M. Hoffman note the merits of talking with those who live through catastrophe: "Methods that privilege narrative and observation, with researchers present and in dialogue with . . . people who must traverse the difficult path between restoration and change . . . are far more appropriate . . . than are more synchronic forms of research"; in *Catastrophe and Culture*, edited by Susanna M. Hoffman and Anthony Oliver-Smith (Santa Fe, NM: School of American Research Press), 12–13.

20. We learned from and were inspired by Carol Stack's classic 1974 study of two urban African American families. Her work endures in part as a testament to that piece of our nature that wants to connect with others we call human, regardless of the barriers societies create to preclude that connection. During nearly three years, Carol, a white woman, forged durable bonds with two poor, urban, black families who opened up their minds and hearts to an anthropologist seeking to make sense

of how people cobble together strategies that allow them to survive with a measure of dignity in the face of hard-wearing poverty; Carol Stack, 1974, *All Our Kin* (New York: Harper and Row); see also Carol Stack, 1996, *Call to Home: African-Americans Reclaim the Rural South* (New York: Basic Books).

CHAPTER 1: "KATRINA TAKES AIM"

1. The epigraph is from Dante Alighieri, 1994, *The Divine Comedy* (New York: Harper), ix.

2. In Brian Handwerk, 2005, "New Orleans Levees Not Built for Worst Case Events," *National Geographic News*, September 2, http://news.nationalgeographic.com/news/2005/09/0902_050902_katrina_levees.html (accessed October 2009). By all accounts Hurricane Katrina was a moderate category 3 storm; it was not a category 4 or 5.

3. An environmental engineer representing the American Academy of Civil Engineers concludes that

> Hurricane Katrina was a catastrophic storm that made landfall in the Gulf Coast near the Louisiana and Mississippi border with wind speeds near 150 mph. But the damage in New Orleans due to the high winds and rain paled in comparison to the devastation resulting from the flooding.

Peter Nicholson, 2005, "Hurricane Katrina: Why Did the Levees Fail?" Testimony before the Senate Committee on Homeland Security and Governmental Affairs, November 5 (Washington, DC: U.S. Congress).

4. Blaise Pascal, in James Byrne, 1997, *Religion and the Enlightenment from Descartes to Kant* (Westminster, England: John Knox Press), 195.

5. Richard Wright, 2008, "Down by the Riverside," in his *Uncle Tom's Children* (New York: HarperCollins), 12.

6. Alfred Schutz with Thomas Luckmann, 1983, *The Structures of the Life World* (Evanston, IL: Northwestern University Press), 2:129.

7. Ibid., 1:11.

8. The language of race was used time and again to parse the alleged distinction between white residents who were "finding" food, medicine, and so on and black residents who were "looting"; Van Jones, 2005, "Black People 'Loot' Food . . . White People 'Find' Food," *Huffington Post*, December, http://www.huffingtonpost.com/van-jones/black-people-loot-food-wh_b_6614.html (accessed September 2007).

9. Claude Lévi-Strauss, 1966, *The Savage Mind* (Chicago: University of Chicago Press). The idea of the *bricoleur* and its connection to people and disaster is explored in Steve Kroll-Smith, Pam Jenkins, and Vern Baxter, 2007, "The Bricoleur and the Possibility of Rescue: First-Responders to the Flooding of New Orleans," *Journal of Public Management and Social Policy* 13(2):5–21.

10. Jamie Doward, Simon English, and Mark Townsend, 2005, "America's Ordeal," *Guardian*, September 3, http://www.guardian.co.uk/world/2005/sep/04/hurricanekatrina.usa (accessed March 2008).

11. Federal Emergency Management Agency (FEMA), 2004, "Hurricane Pam Exercise Concludes," release no. R6-04-093, July 23.

12. U.S. House of Representatives, 2006, "Hurricane Pam," in *A Failure of Initiative*: The Final Report of the Select Bipartisan Committee to Investigate the Preparation for and Response to Hurricane Katrina (Washington, DC: U.S. House of Representatives), http://govinfo.library.unt.edu/katrina/hurricanepam.pdf (accessed March 2008).

13. Walter Maestri, 2005, interview in "The Storm," *Frontline*, September 13, http://www.pbs.org/wgbh/pages/frontline/storm/interviews/maestri.html (accessed August 2007).

14. Michael Brown, 2005, interview in "The Storm," *Frontline*, October 14, http://www.pbs.org/wgbh/pages/frontline/storm/interviews/brown.html (accessed August 2007).

15. In Joby Warrick, 2006, "White House Got Early Warning on Katrina," *Washington Post*, January 24, http://www.washingtonpost.com/wp-dyn/content/article/2006/01/23/AR2006012301711.html (accessed August 2007).

16. In their report to the National Science Foundation, Seed et al. (2006, xx) note,

> Hurricane Katrina has been widely reported to have overwhelmed the eastern side of the New Orleans flood protection system with storm surge and wave loading that exceeded the levels used for design of the system in that area. That is a true statement, but it is also an incomplete view. The storm surge and wave loading at the eastern flank of the New Orleans flood protection system was not vastly greater than design levels, and the carnage that resulted owed much to the inadequacies of the system as it existed at the time of Katrina's arrival. Some overtopping of levees along the eastern flank of the system . . . and also in central areas . . . was inevitable given the design levels authorized by Congress and the surge levels produced in these areas by the actual storm. It does not follow, however, that this overtopping had to result in catastrophic failures and breaching of major portions of the levees protecting these areas, nor the ensuing catastrophic flooding of these populous areas.

CHAPTER 2: GEOGRAPHIES OF CLASS AND COLOR

1. Greater New Orleans Community Data Center, Hollygrove Neighborhood Census 2000, http://www.datacenterresearch.org.

2. Ibid.

3. Terry Eagleton, 2011, *Why Marx Was Right* (New Haven, CT: Yale University Press), 162.

4. More than thirty years ago, William Julius Wilson wrote that the once potent significance of skin color in American society has moderated over time, "so much so that now the life chances of individual blacks have more to do with their economic class position than with their day to day encounters with whites"; William Julius Wilson, 1980, *The Declining Significance of Race: Blacks and Changing American Institutions*, 2nd ed. (Chicago: University of Chicago Press), 1. And writing specifically about class, race, and Hurricane Katrina, Adolph Reed, former New Orleanian and now professor of political science at the University of Pennsylvania, deploys an evocative turn of phrase: it is now possible "to deal black people in and poor people out" of the American dream; Adolph Reed Jr., 2006, introduction to *Unnatural Disaster*, edited by Betsy Reed (New York: Nation Books), xix.

5. Of those Marxists writing today, David Harvey is arguably the most convincing in making the case for the strong tie between material circumstance and the quotidian world of day-to-day life: "It is impossible to sustain the view that capitalism has only a shadowy relation to daily life or that the adjustments or adaptations that occur in daily life are irrelevant for understanding how capital accumulation is working on the world stage"; David Harvey, 2006, *Spaces of Global Capitalism* (London: Verso Press), 80.

6. University of New Orleans Center for Hazard Assessment, Response, and Technology, 2009, "Repetitive Loss Area Analysis #8, City of New Orleans Hollygrove Neighborhood," September 30, http://floodhelp.uno.edu/uploads/Hollygrove%20Area%20Analysis_Final.pdf (accessed November 2010).

7. Lewis Mumford, 1961, *The City in History* (New York: Harcourt, Brace, and World), 461.

8. *Times-Picayune*, 2011, "1955: Pontchartrain Park Opens in New Orleans," November 28, http://www.nola.com/175years/index.ssf/2011/11/1955_pontchartrain_park_opens.html.

9. In E. F. Haas, 1974, *DeLesseps S. Morrison and the Image of Reform: New Orleans Politics, 1946–60* (Baton Rouge: Louisiana State University Press), 75–76.

10. In 1954 the U.S. Supreme Court declared in *Brown v. Topeka Board of Education* that racially separate but equal facilities were illegal.

11. Pontchartrain Park Community Development Corporation, http://www.pontchartrainpark.org/history (accessed April 2009).

12. Ibid.

13. Greater New Orleans Community Data Center, http://www.datacenterresearch.org/data-resources/neighborhood-data/district-6/pontchartrain-park/ (accessed April 2010).

14. T. S. Eliot, 1964, *Murder in the Cathedral* (New York: Harcourt Brace), 69.

15. Clifford Geertz, 1983, *Local Knowledge* (New York: Basic Books), chapter 4.

16. We shamelessly borrow the evocative idea of "telling" from Howard Becker's 2007 *Telling about Society*.

17. William Labov, 1966, "Narrative Analysis: Oral Versions of Personal Experiences," in *Essays on the Verbal and Visual Arts: Proceedings of the American Ethnological Society* (Seattle: American Ethnological Society), 37.

18. Michael Roemer, 1995, *Telling Stories* (Lanham, MD: Rowman and Littlefield), 4.

CHAPTER 3: LIFE ON THE ROAD

1. Kansas Joe McCoy and Memphis Minnie, 1929, "When the Levee Breaks," audio recording, June 18 (New York: Columbia Records).

2. In James West and Chris Vaccaro, 2000, "'Big Easy' a Bowl of Trouble in Hurricanes," *USA Today*, July (republished August 28, 2005), http://www.usatoday.com/weather/news/2000/wnoflood.htm.

3. Gordon Russell, 2005, "Nagin Orders First-Ever Mandatory Evacuation of New Orleans," *Times-Picayune*, August 28, 1.

4. E. L. Quarantelli, 1980, "Evacuation Behavior and Problems," miscellaneous report 27 (Columbus: Disaster Research Center, Ohio State University), 4. See also Thomas Drabek, 1969, "Social Processes in Disaster: Family Evacuation," *Social Problems* 16(3):336–349.

5. Geertz, 1983, 57.

6. Harvey, 2006, 80.

7. Sigmund Freud, quoted in Richard Rorty, 1989, *Contingency, Irony, and Solidarity* (Cambridge, England: Cambridge University Press), 22.

CHAPTER 4: FROM THE ROAD TO EXILE

1. The epigraph is from Dante Alighieri, "Paradise," quoted in María-Inés Lagos-Pope, 1988, *Exile Literature* (Lewisburg, PA: Bucknell University Press), 53–54.

2. For a historical account of hurricanes, people, and evacuations in Louisiana, see David Roth, 2010, *Louisiana Hurricane History* (Camp Spring, MD: National Weather Service), http://www.hpc.ncep.noaa.gov/research/lahur.pdf (accessed March 2011).

3. The brief accounts of Michael and Jesse hint at how the story of Odysseus would need to be complicated considerably if Homer's story, trussed up in modern guise, followed not only a financial consultant but also a tradesman, each seeking a path out of exile. But it would be a Homeric tale worth the telling.

4. Leonardo da Vinci, quoted in Sigmund Freud, 1910/1961, *Leonardo da Vinci and a Memory of His Childhood* (reprint, New York: W. W. Norton), 100.

5. Thomas F. Gieryn, 2000, "A Space for Place in Sociology," *Annual Review of Sociology* 26:463–496; Yi-Fu Tuan, 1977, *Space and Place, the Perspective of Experience* (Minneapolis: University of Minnesota Press).

6. William S. Burroughs, 1990, *Interzone* (New York: Penguin Books). Although Burroughs deploys the word "interzone" to signal a dreamlike state, a time out of time, it is worth noting that the Interzone is also a geographic spot, the International Zone in Tangier, Morocco. Burroughs himself was in exile there for a time after shooting his wife in a drug-crazed moment in Mexico.

7. Mindy T. Fullilove, 1996, "Psychiatric Implications of Displacement: Contributions from the Psychology of Place," *American Journal of Psychiatry* 153:1516–1523.

8. D'Vera Cohn and Rich Morin, 2008, "Who Moves? Who Stays Put? Where's Home?" *Pew Research Social and Demographic Trends*, http://www.pewsocial trends.org (accessed December 2011).

9. U.S. Census Bureau, 2000, American Fact Finder, http://factfinder2.census .gov/faces/nav/jsf/pages/community_facts.xhtml (accessed March 2014).

10. Nathaniel Hawthorne, 1850/1981, *The Scarlet Letter* (reprint, New York: Bantam Books).

11. Benny Turner, 2007, "Katrina Blues," performed by Marva Wright, *After the Levees Broke*, audio recording (Byron Bay, Australia: Aim Records).

12. For a firsthand account of what became the greatest dislocation of an American population since the Dust Bowl, see Lynn Weber and Lori Peek, editors, 2012, *Displaced: Life in the Katrina Diaspora* (Austin: University of Texas Press).

13. In a casual conversation, Kai Erikson recounted a moment when "here" and the subjective "I" join to illustrate the existential idea of place:

> I twice taught at an Austrian town near the Hungarian border called Stradt-schleining. It had once been a part of Hungary. I used to spend time in the town square and was told of the following happening. A sociologist was asking people around the square that old question "Where are you from?" He had hoped to learn how many of the old folk there thought of themselves as Austrian and how many as Hungarian. The first man he approached was asked that question and appeared to be flabbergasted: "Well," he said, looking around for help, "I'm from . . . from . . . I'm from here!"

14. Alfred Schutz, 1999, *On Phenomenology and Social Relations* (Chicago: University of Chicago Press), 27.

15. Fullilove, 1996.

16. Edward Relph, 1976, *Place and Placelessness* (London: Pion Books).

17. A notable exception is the noteworthy volume edited by Weber and Peek, 2012.

18. Jean-Paul Sartre, in Christina Howells, *The Cambridge Companion to Sartre* (Cambridge, England: Cambridge University Press), 48. Sartre conjures the image of "metastable" to warn of the dangers of personal collapse. We can live only so long in a precarious, unstable, and transitory world.

19. There are no fixed numbers on the average time people spent out of their houses, but one study found that fourteen months after the flood, 38 percent of the displaced in Louisiana had not returned to their properties. Among the people we interviewed, the shortest time anyone spent away from home was three months,

and the longest was more than three years. Some extended family members have not returned at all; Jeffrey A. Groen and Anne E. Polivka, 2008, "Hurricane Katrina Evacuees: Who They Are, Where They Are, and How They Are Faring," *Monthly Labor Review*, March (Washington, DC: U.S. Department of Labor, Bureau of Labor Statistics), http://www.bls.gov/opub/mlr/2008/03/art3full.pdf (accessed July 2012).

CHAPTER 5: IT'S AVAILABLE, BUT IS IT ACCESSIBLE?

1. The epigraph is from Vincanne Adams, 2012, "The Other Road to Serfdom: Recovery by the Market and the Affect Economy in New Orleans," *Public Culture* 24(1): 192.

2. George W. Bush, 2005, "President Discusses Hurricane Relief in Address to the Nation", September 15 (Washington, DC: White House), http://georgewbush -whitehouse.archives.gov/news/releases/2005/09/20050915-8.html (accessed October 2006).

3. Ibid.

4. Herbert Hoover, *American Individualism* (New York: Doubleday).

5. Lewis Carroll, 1865/2008, *Alice's Adventures in Wonderland* (republished, Amazon: CreateSpace), 89.

6. C. W. Mills, 1959, *The Sociological Imagination* (Oxford, England: Oxford University Press).

7. Gordon Thomas and Max M. Witts, 1971, *The San Francisco Earthquake* (New York: Stein and Day), 66.

8. Tom Graham, 1961, "Sunday Interview—Gladys Hansen, 90 Years Later, Quake Victims Get Names," *San Francisco Chronicle*, April 14; see also Simon Winchester, 2005, *The Crack at the Edge of the World: America and the Great California Earthquake of 1906* (New York: Harper).

9. Christoph Strupp, 2006, "Dealing with Disaster: The San Francisco Earthquake of 1906," paper presented at the symposium "San Francisco Earthquake 1906: Urban Reconstruction, Insurance, and Implications for the Future," Institute of European Studies, University of California Berkeley, March 22.

10. Marie Bolton, 1997, "Recovery for Whom? Social Conflict after the San Francisco Earthquake and Fire, 1906–1915," PhD diss., University of California, Davis.

11. U.S. Congress, 1970, *Laws and Concurrent Resolutions Enacted during the First Session of the Ninety-first Congress of the United States of America*, vol. 83, part 1, Statutes at Large (Washington, DC: Government Printing Office), 124–129; see also R. H. Platt, 1999, *Disasters and Democracy: The Politics of Extreme Natural Events* (Washington, DC: Island Press).

12. FEMA, 2007, "Individual and Public Assistance: Both Important to the Louisiana Recovery Process," FEMA release no. 1603-263, January 6, http://www .fema.gov/news-release/2006/01/06/individual-and-public-assistance-both -important-louisiana-recovery-process (accessed February 2008).

13. FEMA, 2007, FEMA Public Assistance Guide, http://www.fema.gov/public -assistance-policy-and-guidance/public-assistance-guide (accessed October 2007).

14. Ibid.

15. Income figures are from U.S. Census Bureau, 2000, Demographic Profiles, Census 2000, http://censtats.census.gov/pub/Profiles.shtml (accessed March 2009).

16. In Friedrich Nietzsche, 1885/1999, *Thus Spoke Zarathustra* (reprint, New York: Dover), 11.

17. Roosevelt spoke these words on January 20, 1937; quoted in H. W. Brands, 2008, *Traitor to His Class: The Privileged Life and Radical Presidency of Franklin Delano Roosevelt* (New York: Doubleday), 457.

18. Ayn Rand, 1962, "Who Will Protect Us from Our Protectors?" *Objectivist Newsletter*, May 17.

19. In Scotty Shane and Eric Lipton, 2005, "Stumbling Storm-Aid Effort Put Tons of Ice on Trips to Nowhere," *New York Times*, October 1.

20. In History Commons, 2001, "FEMA Director Plans to Reduce FEMA's Role in Disaster Mitigation and Prevention," May 15, http://www.historycommons.org /timeline.jsp?katrina_policies_that_affected_intensity_of_katrina_impact=katrina _femaRestructuring&timeline=hurricane_katrina_tmln (accessed March 2002).

21. Jeanne M. Lambrew and Donna E. Shalala, 2006, "Federal Health Policy to Hurricane Katrina, What It Was and What It Could Have Been," *Journal of the American Medical Association* 296(11): 394–397.

22. U.S. Senator John Sununu, 2005, Sununu Senate Floor Remarks regarding Proposed $9 Billion Expansion of Medicaid Program, September 27 (Washington, DC: U.S. Senate), http://sununu.senate.gov/floor_statements9-27-05 (accessed September 2006).

23. Gordon Russell and James Varney, 2005, "From Blue Tarps to Debris Removal, Layers of Contractors Drive up the Cost of Recovery, Critics Say," *Times Picayune*, December 29, http://www.pulitzer.org/archives/7090 (accessed August 2014).

24. It is worth noting that Paul Ryan, the vice-presidential nominee on the Republican ticket in 2012, is a disciple of Ayn Rand; Brad Plumer, 2012, "What Did Ayn Rand Teach Paul Ryan about Monetary Policy?" *Washington Post*, August 13, http://www.washingtonpost.com/blogs/ezra-klein/wp/2012/08/13/what-did-ayn -rand-teach-paul-ryan-about-monetary-policy (accessed September 2012).

25. Road Home Program, "The Road Home, Building a Safer, Stronger, Smarter Louisiana," https://road2la.org/ (accessed June 2012).

26. ICF International, 2006, "ICF International Awarded Major Contract to Help Rebuild Louisiana Housing Infrastructure" (Fairfax, VA: ICF International), http://www.icfi.com/news/2006/icf-awarded-major-contract-rebuild-louisiana -housing-infrastructure (accessed June 2007).

27. Vincanne Adams, 2012, 186. See also Vincanne Adams, 2013, *Markets of Sorry, Labors of Faith* (Durham, NC: Duke University Press).

28. David Hammer, 2007, "Indecision Clogging Road Home," *Times-Picayune*, February 19.

29. Frank Silvestri, 2007, Testimony in Senate Hearing 10-249, "The Road Home? An Examination of the Goals, Costs, Management, and Impediments Facing Louisiana's Road Home Program," May 24 (Washington, DC: GPO), http://www.gpo.gov/fdsys/pkg/CHRG-110shrg36609/html/CHRG-110shrg36609.htm (accessed February 2012).

30. Hammer, 2007.

31. Adams, 2013, 88.

32. In John Moreno Gonzales, 2008, "Katrina Victims Complain about Red Tape," Associated Press, published in *USA Today*, March 3, http://www.usatoday.com/news/nation/2008-03-13-4205913428_x.htm (accessed January 2009). The word "entitlement" was, at one time, a neutral label for federal spending on social programs. It is now often used by Republicans to signal that government programs to assist the poor are encouraging people to stay poor and collect their "entitlements"; David Lynch, 2013, "Obama Programs Derided by Republicans as Pejorative Entitlements," *Bloomberg*, April 15, http://www.bloomberg.com/news/2013-04-15/obama-programs-derided-by-republicans-as-pejorative-entitlements.html (accessed April 2013).

33. The term "moral hazard" is part of the vernacular of the insurance industry. It has at least two meanings. It might refer to the motivation of a beneficiary to engage in riskier behaviors because she knows she is covered by a policy. It might also mean an individual asks the insurer to pay for more of the harmful consequences of a behavior than otherwise would have been the case. The ICF spokeswoman is referring to this second meaning. An article in the *New York Times* notes that many Americans were outraged at the behavior of victims of Hurricane Katrina who "were spending disaster relief, paid by taxpayers, on tattoos, $800 handbags and trips to topless bars"; Shaila Dewan, 2012, "Moral Hazard: A Tempest-Tossed Idea," *New York Times*, February 26. This fable, like the one of mass looting in the emergency phase of the disaster, is part of the mythology of Miss Katrina. On the concept of moral hazard, see Mark V. Pauly, 1968, "The Economics of the Moral Hazard: Comment," *American Economic Review* 50(3): 531–537.

34. In U.S. District Court of the District of Columbia, 2006, ACORN v. FEMA, Case 1:06-cv-01521-RJL, Document 17, November 29.

35. Merriam-Webster, "Kafkaesque," http://www.merriam-webster.com/dictionary/kafkaesque (accessed February 2009).

36. Mark Waller, 2013, "Hurricane Katrina Eight Years Later, a Statistical Snapshot of the New Orleans Area," *Times-Picayune*, September 3, http://www.nola.com/katrina/index.ssf/2013/08/hurricane_katrina_eight_years.htm (accessed March 2014).

37. Arthur Schopenhauer, quoted in Joseph Campbell, 1991, *The Power of Myth* (New York: Anchor Books), 168.

38. Michael A. Fletcher, 2011, "HUD to Pay $62 Million to La. Homeowners to

Settle Road Home Lawsuit," *Washington Post*, July 6, http://www.washingtonpost
.com/business/economy/hud-to-pay-62-million-to-la-homeowners-to-settle
-road-home-lawsuit/2011/07/06/gIQAtsFN1H_story.html (accessed March 2012).

39. William James, 1892/1983, *Psychology: Briefer Course* (Cambridge: Harvard University Press), 372.

40. Lewis Carroll, 1865/2008, chapter 7, "A Mad Tea Party."

CHAPTER 6: REBUILDING IN A BROKEN CITY

1. Jackson Browne, 1976, "The Pretender," on his album *The Pretender* (Hollywood, CA: Sound Factory).

2. Rebecca Mowbray, 2006, "Wounded N.O. Economy Remains in Coma," *Times-Picayune*, August 25.

3. Ibid.

4. Amy Liu, Matt Fellowes, and Mia Mabanta, 2006, *A One-Year Review of Key Indicators of Recovery in Post-Storm New Orleans*, special edition of *The Katrina Index* (Washington, DC: Brookings Institution Press); Robin Rudowitz, Diane Rowland, and Adele Shartzer, 2006, "Health Care in New Orleans before and after Hurricane Katrina," *Health Affairs* 25, no. 5 (November): 393–406.

5. Anna Livia Brand and Karl Seidman, 2008, "Assessing Post-Katrina Recovery in New Orleans: Recommendations for Equitable Rebuilding," report (Boston: Community Innovators Lab, Department of Urban Studies and Planning, Massachusetts Institute of Technology), 2–3, http://web.mit.edu/colab/pdf/papers/Assessing_PostKatrina_Recovery.pdf (accessed December 2009).

6. Lawrence N. Powell, 2007, "What Does American History Tell Us about Katrina and Vice Versa?" *Journal of American History* 94 (December), special issue, *Through the Eye of Katrina*, 863–876.

7. Liu, Fellowes, and Mabanta, 2006, 7.

8. Allen M. Johnson Jr. and Campbell Robertson, 2014, "10-Year Term on Graft Charges for C. Ray Nagin, Former Mayor of New Orleans," *New York Times*, July 14.

9. Ted Cushman, 2010, "FEMA House Elevation Grants Cause Controversy," *Journal of Light Construction* (November), http://www.jlconline.com/coastal -contractor/fema-house-elevation-grants-cause-controversy.aspx (accessed August 2011).

10. FEMA, 2014, "Increased Cost of Compliance," http://www.fema.gov/national -flood-insurance-program-2/increased-cost-compliance-coverage; FEMA, 2014, "The National Flood Insurance Program," http://www.fema.gov/national-flood -insurance-program (accessed February 2014). FEMA continuously updates its web pages.

11. Edward J. Blakely, 2012, *My Storm, Managing the Recovery of New Orleans in the Wake of Katrina* (Philadelphia: University of Pennsylvania Press), 3.

12. Bring New Orleans Back Commission (BNOB), Urban Planning Commit-

tee, 2006, "Action Plan for New Orleans: The New American City," Parks and Open Space Plan (New Orleans: BNOB), http://www.npr.org/documents/2006/jan/City PlanningFinalReport.pdf (accessed March 2010).

13. Adam Nossister, 2007, "Steering New Orleans' Recovery with a Clinical Eye," *New York Times*, April 10.

14. In Nicolai Ouroussoff, 2006, "In New Orleans, Each Resident Is Master of Plan to Rebuild," *New York Times*, August 8.

15. Ariella Cohen, 2011, "Despite Health Fears, Trailers Are Housing Disaster Victims," *The Lens*, May 19, http://thelensnola.org/2011/05/19/fema-trailers -formaldehyde-katrina-rita-tuscaloosa-tornadoe/ (accessed August 2011).

16. Ouroussoff, 2006.

17. Allison Plyer, 2012, "Facts for Features: Hurricane Katrina Impact," Greater New Orleans Community Data Center, August 10, http://www.gnocdc.org/Facts forfeatures/HurricaneKatrinaImpact/index.html (accessed August 2012).

18. Philip Mattera, n.d., "Profiles of 12 Companies That Have Received Large Contracts for Cleanup and Reconstruction Work Related to Hurricanes Katrina and Rita" (Washington, DC: Corporate Research Project/Good Jobs First).

19. Sigmund Freud, 1930/1961, *Civilization and Its Discontents* (reprint, New York: W. W. Norton), 37–38.

20. The case for relief and rebuilding creating a "second disaster" in many of the city's African American neighborhoods is convincingly made by Robert Bullard in a short bullet-point essay enumerating the varied ways in which what is done in the name of "disaster recovery" might well become a calamitous misadventure, a tragedy in its own right; Robert Bullard, "Katrina and the Second Disaster: A Twenty-Point Plan to Destroy Black New Orleans" (Atlanta: Environmental Justice Resource Center, Clark Atlanta University), http://www.ejrc.cau.edu /Bullard20PointPlan.html (accessed July 2012). A comparative inquiry into the 1906 San Francisco earthquake and fire and the 2005 flooding of New Orleans builds a more complex, historical version of this argument; Steve Kroll-Smith and Shelly Brown-Jeffy, 2013, "A Tale of Two American Cities: Disaster, Class, and Citizenship in San Francisco 1906 and New Orleans 2005," *Journal of Historical Sociology* 26(4): 527–551.

CHAPTER 7: "THE KATRINA EFFECT"

1. Leysia Palen, S. Vieweg, J. Sutton, S. B. Liu, and A. Hughes, 2007, "Crisis Informatics: Studying Crisis in a Networked World," paper presented at the Third International Conference on e-Social Science, Ann Arbor, MI, October 7–9. From the standard reference text in the field, *Handbook on Disaster Research*, to the most recent FEMA *National Disaster Recovery Framework*, with its "scalable, flexible and adaptable coordinating structures to . . . promote effective Federal recovery assistance," recovery appears as the final outcome in the human experience of catas-

trophe; Havidan Rodriguez, E. L. Quarantelli, and Russell Dynes, editors, 2006, *Handbook of Disaster Research* (New York: Springer); FEMA, 2011, *National Disaster Recovery Framework: Strengthening Disaster Recovery for the Nation*, September, http://www.fema.gov/pdf/recoveryframework/ndrf.pdf.

2. "The past is never dead. It's not even past"; William Faulkner, 1951/1975, *Requiem for a Nun* (reprint, New York: Vintage), Act 1, Scene 3.

3. Genesis 8:20.

4. Genesis 9:20.

5. John Stuart Mill, 1848/2004, *Principles of Political Economy, with Some of Their Applications to Social Philosophy* (reprint, Indianapolis, IN: Hackett), book I, chapter 5, paragraph 19.

6. J. Eavey and R. C. Ratard, 2008, "Post-Katrina Mortality in the Greater New Orleans Area, Louisiana," *Journal of Louisiana State Medical Society* 160, no. 5 (September–October): 267–272.

7. Charles Wellford, Brenda J. Bond, and Sean Goodison, 2011, "Crime in New Orleans: Analyzing Crime Trends and New Orleans' Responses to Crime," March 15, http://www.nolaoig.org/uploads/File/All/BJA_report_on_crime.pdf (accessed June 2013).

8. Adams, 2013, 4.

9. *Times-Picayune*, 2010, *New Orleans Crime Index*, May, http://www.nola.com/crime/index.ssf/2010/05/ (accessed March 2010).

10. Steve Kroll-Smith and Stephen R. Couch, 1993, "Symbols, Ecology, and Contamination: Case Studies in the Ecological-Symbolic Approach to Disaster," *Research in Social Problems and Public Policy* 5:47–73.

11. This memorable observation is attributed to Anaïs Nin, though no one has found it in any of her published work; in Herb Cohen, 1982, *You Can Negotiate Anything* (New York: Bantam Books), 159.

12. For a close look at how the perceptions of neighbors and neighborhood shape a person's understanding of whether he or she has recovered from disaster, see Kai Erikson's 1976 definitive account of the Buffalo Creek flood, *Everything in Its Path* (New York: Simon and Schuster), 186–245.

13. On the long-term anthropogenic causes of disaster, see the now classic 1994 piece by Anthony Oliver-Smith, "Peru's Five-Hundred-Year Earthquake: Vulnerability in Historical Context," in *Disasters, Development, and Environment*, edited by A. Varley (Chichester, England: John Wiley and Sons), 3–48.

14. Richard Rorty, 1989.

15. Herbert Blumer might call editing a "sensitizing concept"; Herbert Blumer, "What Is Wrong with Social Theory," *American Sociological Review* 18 (1954): 3–10.

16. Natasha Trethewey, 2010, *Beyond Katrina* (Athens: University of Georgia Press), 103.

17. In Eliott C. McLaughlin, 2006, "No More Hurricane Katrinas," CNN, May 19, http://articles.cnn.com/2006-04-06/weather/hurricane.names_1_storm-names -hurricane-names-hurricane-status?_s=PM:WEATHER (accessed March 2013).

1. The epigraph is from Friedrich Nietzsche, 1882/2001, *The Gay Science* (Cambridge, England: Cambridge University Press), 355.

2. James, 1890/1950, 1:462.

3. Dennis Wrong, 1961, "The Oversocialized Conception of Man in Modern Sociology," *American Sociology Review* 26(2): 184.

4. Perrow, 1982, 686.

5. In Ralph Barton Perry, 1996, *The Thought and Character of William James* (Nashville, TN: Vanderbilt University Press), 96.

6. Terry Eagleton, 2007, *How to Read a Poem* (Malden, MA: Wiley-Blackwell), 20.

7. Daniel P. Aldrich, 2012, *Building Resilience: Social Capital in Post-Disaster Recovery* (Chicago: University of Chicago Press); Committee on Increasing National Resilience to Hazards and Disasters, 2012, *Disaster Resilience, a National Imperative* (Washington, DC: National Academies Press).

8. Committee on Increasing National Resilience to Hazards and Disasters, 2012, 1.

9. This text is from a field note written April 4, 1983; see Steve Kroll-Smith and Steve Couch, 2009, *The Real Disaster Is above Ground*, 2nd ed. (Lexington: University Press of Kentucky).

10. A recent article by anthropologist Roberto Barrios sounds the theme we are stressing in our short critique of resilience; Robert Barrios, 2014, "'Here, I'm not at Ease': Anthropological Perspectives on Community Resilience," *Disasters* 38(2): 329–350.

11. For a magisterial account of how businesses and government agencies create elaborate plans to assure an effective and orderly response to disaster that have little or no chance of succeeding, see Lee Clarke, 2001, *Mission Impossible, Using Fantasy Documents to Tame Disaster* (Chicago: University of Chicago Press).

ABOUT THE AUTHORS AND SERIES EDITOR

STEVE KROLL-SMITH is currently a professor of sociology at the University of North Carolina, Greensboro. He was formerly a research professor at the University of New Orleans.

VERN BAXTER is professor and chair of the Department of Sociology at the University of New Orleans.

PAM JENKINS is a research professor of sociology and a faculty member in the women's studies program at the University of New Orleans.

KAI ERIKSON, SERIES EDITOR, is Professor Emeritus of Sociology and American Studies at Yale University. He is a past president of the American Sociological Association, winner of the MacIver and Sorokin Awards from the ASA, author of *A New Species of Trouble: Explorations in Disaster, Trauma, and Community*, and his research and teaching interests include American communities, human disasters, and ethnonational conflict.

INDEX

Page numbers in **boldface** refer to figures, tables, maps, and photographs.

city bus service (New Orleans), 101
city council. *See* New Orleans City
    Council
civic responsibility: and American indi-
    vidualism, 80–81
class: fortunes of, eclipsed by chance, 34;
    limitations and possibilities of, 33;
    and New Orleans' neighborhoods,
    31, 32. *See also* Hollygrove; Pontchar-
    train Park
collectivism, 80, 92; versus individual-
    ism, 89–93
contingency: chance, material well-being,
    and the shadow of, 53, 62, 63; and life
    in exile, 75
contractors and subcontractors, 107; and
    FEMA trailers, 86; and fraud, 102; and
    homeowners and rebuilding efforts,
    107–114; and Operation Blue Roof, 91
conversation: and significance of first-
    person narratives on disaster, 6–7,
    141n13
crisis counseling, 84

Da Vinci, Leonardo: and the countless
    causes of ordinary life, 64
Davis-Bacon Act, 90–91
demographics: of New Orleans' neigh-
    borhoods, 31–32. *See also* Hollygrove;
    Pontchartrain Park
diaspora: and Hurricane Katrina, 69,
    146n12
disaster: anthropological views on, 8–9,
    141n19; and assessment in 2000 of
    potential damage of severe hurri-
    cane, 51; chance and unpredictability
    in the study of, 133–137; and disaster-
    assistance culture, 7; etymology of,
    meaning "bad star," 136; and the sig-
    nificance of conversation on, 6–7,
    141n13; social science of, 1–2. *See also*
    chance; contingency; disaster assis-
    tance; disaster recovery; place; space
disaster assistance: 75, 81, 82; and eligi-
    bility, 83–89; and formula for calculat-
    ing rebuilding costs, 97; government
    efforts to minimize role in response

to Hurricane Katrina, 90–91; and
    the Kafkaesque bureaucratic maze,
    79–80, 85–89, 93–97; and Mad Hatter
    parallel, 98; miscarriages of, toward
    low-income African American home-
    owners, 97–98; and parallel to Alice's
    adventures in Wonderland, 81, 95, 98;
    politics of, 80–82, 90–93; privatiza-
    tion of, 91–92; and the San Francisco
    earthquake and fire of 1906, 83. *See
    also* disaster; disaster recovery; Dis-
    aster Relief Act (1950); Federal Emer-
    gency Management Agency (FEMA);
    individual assistance (IA) funding;
    National Flood Insurance Program;
    Louisiana Recovery Authority (LRA);
    Operation Blue Roof; public assis-
    tance (PA) funding; Public Law 91-79
    (1969); Road Home Program
disaster planning, 1–2, 29–30
disaster recovery, 115, 127, 128, 152n12; as
    an abstraction, 129; and "editing" life
    post-Katrina, 129–132; and the human
    experience of catastrophe, 116–118,
    151n1; and PTSD and the lived ex-
    perience of trauma, 120–123; and
    residents' appraisals on the "Katrina
    effect," 118–122, 123–124, 125, 127, 128,
    129, 130, 131–132; and resilience of
    community, 136–137, 153n10. *See also*
    disaster; disaster assistance; "Katrina
    effect," the
Disaster Relief Act (1950), 83
disaster unemployment payments, 84
discrimination: and African American
    homeowners' class-action lawsuit
    against Road Home Program, 97–98
displacement. *See* exile
Du Bois, W.E.B.: and double-
    consciousness, xi

earthquake. *See* San Francisco 1906
    earthquake and fire
elevation: homeowners and the "eleva-
    tion grant game," 102–104; of New
    Orleans, 5, 28, 36
eligibility: and federal disaster assistance,

83–89; for individual assistance (IA) funding, 84–85; for public assistance (PA) funding, 84. *See also* disaster assistance

Eliot, T. S., 46

Entergy: and FEMA trailers, 86

entitlement: and government social programs, 92, 149n32; and variations on meaning, 149n32

Erikson, Kai: on the existential idea of "place," 71, 72, 146n13

evacuation: and displacement, 75, 146n19; and experience-distant vantage point, 52, 53; and Hollygrove residents, 51–52, 53, 54, 57–60, 62–64, 65; and importance of family, 60–61; and initial travel plans of evacuees, 62–63, 64, 70, 73; and the link between contingency and material well-being, 62; and mandatory order for, xi–xii, 51; and orderliness, 52; and the parallel to Odysseus's travels, 64; planning for, 51; and Pontchartrain Park residents, 54–55, 56, 63, 65, 70; and the role of "space," 64–65

exile: and absence of "place," 65–66, 68; and displacement, 75, 146n19; and the existential place of "here," 71, 72, 146n13; and Hollygrove residents, 65, 67, 69, 73–74; and the "interzone," 65, 146n6; and Jean-Paul Sartre's "metastable," 75, 146n18; and place, 64–65; and Pontchartrain Park residents, 65, 67–68, 69, 70–71, 72; and the scarlet letter "E," 66–68

Faulkner, William: on the past haunting the present, 116, 152n2

federal aid. *See* disaster assistance; Federal Emergency Management Agency (FEMA)

Federal Emergency Management Agency (FEMA), 1–2; congressional investigation into federal response to Hurricane Katrina, 90; and damage assessments process, 104–105, 106; and Hollygrove disaster assistance narratives, 86–88, 88–89; and "Hurricane Pam" risk assessment exercise, 29–30; and government efforts to minimize federal role in response to Hurricane Katrina, 90–91; and house elevation grants, 103, 104; and Judge Richard Leon on "Kafkaesque applications," 93; and the Kafkaesque bureaucratic maze, 79–82, 93; and Operation Blue Roof, 91; and Pontchartrain Park disaster assistance narratives, 81–82, 85, 86, 87, 89; seeking disaster assistance from, and the parallel to Alice's adventures in Wonderland, 81, 95, 98. *See also* Kafkaesque; Road Home Program

federal government: role of, in catastrophes, 80–81, 82, 83

FEMA trailers, 85, 86, 101, 103, 106

"first-day strangeness," and the Mississippi River flood of 1927, 18–19

flooding: aerial view of New Orleans, **21**; and levee protection, 17, 143n16; Mississippi River flood of 1927, 18–19; New Orleans as Atlantis underwater, 63; Old Testament flood, 1, 116–117

flood insurance, 75; and "elevation grant game," 102–104; and National Flood Insurance Program, 91

food stamps, 84

French Quarter: as an "island," 28

Freud, Sigmund: on chance, 57; on civilization and social processes, 114–115

Gay Science, The (Nietzsche), 133

Geertz, Clifford, 7, 47, 52

Gentilly (neighborhood): and the "Katrina effect," 120

God: and the biblical flood, 1

go-it-alone attitude, 48, 105, 106–107. *See also* homeowners; rebuilding

government assistance: politics of, 80–82, 90–93. *See also* disaster assistance; Federal Emergency Management Agency (FEMA); Kafkaesque

Greater New Orleans Fair Housing Action Center, 97

Greater New Orleans Foundation (GNOF), 106
Great Flood of 1927. *See* Mississippi River flood of 1927
green dots, as future green spaces, 105. *See also* Bring New Orleans Back
gypsy contractors, 107. *See also* contractors and subcontractors; rebuilding

Harvey, David: on material circumstance and impact on daily life, 33, 144n5
Hazard Mitigation Grant Program, 104, 106
Health and Human Services, 91
health care, 91
Hobsbawm, Eric: on the familiar and routine to the mysterious and disorderly, 6
Hollygrove: abandoned houses post-Katrina, **124**; African American entertainers from, 32; as an African American working-class neighborhood, 5, 133; demographic changes in, 2000–2010, 123–125, **126**; demographics of, 31–32, 38–41; description of neighborhood, 35–41; on differences in material circumstances, 33–34; and evacuation narratives, 62–64; and exile narratives, 67, 73–74; family and connection to place, 65–66; FEMA and disaster assistance narratives, 79–80, 86–88, 88–89; first-person narratives on Katrina evacuation, 51–52, 53, 54, 57–60, 61; geography of, 35–38; history of, xii, 32, 36, 38–39; homeowners inspecting flood-damaged homes narratives, 99–100; housing styles of, 36; and the "Katrina effect," 120–122, 128; living in exile and the scarlet letter "E," 66–68; map of, **35**, **37**; narratives on rebuilding and contractors, 108–110, 111, 112–114; navigating the "Kafkaesque" bureaucracy of the Road Home Program, 93, 94–95; and overview of first-person narratives, 46–48; and personal perspectives on race, 11–12; and quality of neighbor-

hood life post-Katrina, 123–125; rebuilding narratives, 107, 108–110, 111, 112–114; rebuilt house post-Katrina, **110**; recovering and "editing" life post-Katrina, 129–132; riding out the storm narratives, 19, 22, 26–28
Holy Cross (New Orleans neighborhood), 107
home: the strangeness of, post-Katrina, 128–129. *See also* place
homeowners: and African American homeowners' class-action lawsuit against Road Home Program, 97–98; dealing with contractors and rebuilding, 107–114; and Road Home Program, 80, 84, 87, 89, 91–92, 93–97; rebuilding and "go-it-alone" attitude, 105, 106–107; seeking disaster assistance and the parallels to Alice's adventures in Wonderland, 81, 95. *See also* "Katrina effect," the; Road Home Program
homeowners' insurance, 75
Hoover, Herbert: and American individualism, 80
Housing and Urban Development (HUD), 97
housing rehab grants. *See* Road Home Program
human suffering, 141n13
Hurricane Betsy, 4
Hurricane Katrina, 133–134, 137; and City of New Orleans' lack of urban recovery plans, 101–102, 108; comparison with San Francisco earthquake and fire of 1906, 105, 151n20; congressional investigation into federal response to, 90; and creation of a post-positivist world, 135–136; description of flood-damaged homes, 99–100; and the diaspora, 69, 146n12; and disaster assistance, 79–82, 84; and government efforts to minimize role in response to, 90–91; initial lack of resources, 69; and the "Katrina effect," 118, 119, 120–123, 125, **126**, 127, 128–129; and the legacy of, 117, 132; landfall, 17; and mandatory evacua-

tion order, xi–xii, 51; mythology of, 149n33; New Orleans mortality rates post-Katrina, 120; personification of, as "Miss Katrina," 5; race and response to, 45–46; recovery and the "editing" of life post-Katrina, 129–131; retirement of "Katrina" as a hurricane name, 132; and Sigmund Freud on civilization, 114–115; and storm surges, 17, 20. *See also* Hollygrove; Pontchartrain Park

Hurricane Pam (FEMA risk assessment exercise), 29–30

Hurricane Rita, 17, 84; impact of, on New Orleans post-Katrina, 6

ICF International: and Louisiana Recovery Act (LRA), 91, 92; and "moral hazard," 92, 149n33

increased cost of compliance (ICC) grant, 104

indeterminism: William James on, 134

individual assistance (IA) funding, 84, 85, 89. *See also* disaster assistance; Public Law 91-79 (1969)

individualism, 80, 92; versus collectivism, 89–93

Inner City Fund (ICF), 91–92

insecurity. *See* zone of insecurity

insurance companies: flood insurance, 75; homeowners' insurance, 75; "moral hazard" term as defined by insurance industry, 92, 149n33; National Flood Insurance Program, 91; navigating the bureaucratic red tape of, 75

interzone: life in exile and the, 65, 146n6

Jackson Square: George W. Bush's address at, 80, 90

James, William: on human nature and chance, 134, 135; and the out of the ordinary, 2; and personification of natural disasters, 140n11; and zone of insecurity, 2

Kafka, Franz, 79, 93

Kafkaesque: getting through the maze

of federal disaster assistance, 79–80, 85–89, 93–97. *See also* disaster assistance; Federal Emergency Management Agency (FEMA); Hollygrove; Pontchartrain Park; Road Home Program

"Katrina effect," the, 118, 119, 120–123, 125, **126**, 127, 128–129. *See also* disaster recovery; Hollygrove; Pontchartrain Park; rebuilding

Katrina Index project, 102

Labov, William, 48

Lake Pontchartrain: and the levee height, 4, **5**

Lakeview (New Orleans neighborhood), 107

Leavitt, Michael, 91

legal services, 84

Leon, U.S. District Court Judge Richard: on FEMA's "Kafkaesque" application process, 93

levee system, 4, 6; and breaches, 17; and protection system, 17, 143n16; and the Road Home Program, 91. *See also* Lake Pontchartrain; Mississippi River; New Orleans

Lévi-Strauss, Claude: and the *bricoleur* in disaster, 28, 81, 142n9

literature: slavery as depicted in, xi

Liu, Amy: on New Orleans' non-functioning government, 102

looting: and language of race, 142n8

Louisiana Recovery Authority (LRA), 97; and no-bid contract with ICF International, 91

Mad Hatter parallel, and providing documentation for disaster assistance, 98

Maestri, Walter, 51

Markets of Sorrow (Adams), 120

material well-being: and chance, 53, 57, 133–134; choices and contingencies shaped by, during disaster, 33–34; and the compassion of others, 64; and the material resource term "cheese" in the black community, 53–54, 57, 60,

61; and place and placelessness, 74; and the shadow of contingency and chance, 62

Medicaid health coverage, 91

medical facilities (New Orleans), 101

metastable: Sartre on, and the exiled world, 75, 146n18

Mid-City (neighborhood), and the "Katrina effect," 119–120

middle-class neighborhood. *See* Ponchartrain Park

Mill, John Stuart: on human nature and disaster, 117

Mississippi River: and the levee height, 4, 5; and slavery, xi

Mississippi River flood of 1927, 18

Miss Katrina, 119, 132; and disaster and chance, 136, 137; as Faulkner's "past" haunting the present, 116, 152n2; mythology of, 149n33; personification of Hurricane Katrina as, 5

Moody's: and New Orleans as a dormant city, 101

moral hazard, as defined by insurance industry, 92, 149n33

Morial, Ernest "Dutch," 32, 42

Morial, Mark, 32

Morrison, deLesseps Story, 41–42

Mumford, Lewis, 38

Nagin, Ray, xi, xii, 51, 102, 106

National Fair Housing Alliance, 97

National Flood Insurance Program (NFIP): and flooding mitigation measures, 91, 103, 104. *See also* insurance companies

natural disasters: personification of, 5, 140n11

New Orleans: as the "accidental city," 3; aerial view of flooding, 21; antebellum, xi; as Atlantis underwater, 63; and Bienville's "l'isle de la Nouvelle Orléans," 3; as a "city in a bowl," 4, 5, 17, 28; as a "city in a coma," 101; city's damage-determination process, 104–105; first mandatory evacuation order issued for the city, 51; ground

elevations, 4, 5; history of flooding, 4; lack of disaster recovery plans post-Katrina, 101–102, 108; and mortality rates post-Katrina, 120; neighborhoods by class and race, 31–32; and poverty line, xi–xii; rebuilding efforts, 107–114; and recovery process at one-year anniversary of Katrina, 101–102; unpopular urban revitalization plan post-Katrina, 105–106. *See also* Bring New Orleans Back; Greater New Orleans Foundation (GNOF); Hollygrove; Hurricane Katrina; Pontchartrain Park

New Orleans City Council, 102–104

New York Times: on rebuilding efforts of New Orleans residents, 106–107

Nietzsche, Friedrich, 86, 133

Noah, and the biblical flood, 116–117

no-bid contract, 91

Northup, Solomon, xi

Odysseus's travels, and parallel to New Orleans residents' evacuation and exile, 64

Old Testament biblical flood, 1, 116–117

Oliver-Smith, Anthony: on interviewing disaster survivors, 141n19

Operation Blue Roof, 91

oral tradition: slavery and, xi

pain. *See* human suffering

Pascal, Blaise: on ordinary life, 18

past, the: Miss Katrina and Faulkner's "the past is never dead," 116, 152n2

Perrow, Charles: on social order and randomness of everyday life, 134–135

personification: of Hurricane Katrina as "Miss Katrina," 5; of natural disasters, 5, 140n11

Philippe, Duc d'Orléans, 3

Philips-Jordan (federal contractor), 107

place: and exile, 64–65; and the existential "here," 71, 72, 146n13; contingency of, 75; family and connection to, 65–66; and placelessness of, 72–74; search for a temporary, 79; the security of, 65; and the strangeness of home post-Katrina, 128–129. *See also* evacuation; exile; home

Plessy, Homer Adolph, xii

Plessy v. Ferguson, xii

politics: of federal disaster assistance, 80–82, 90–93. *See also* Brown, Michael; Bush, George W.; civic responsibility; collectivism; Davis-Bacon Act; disaster assistance; Federal Emergency Management Agency (FEMA); individualism

Pontchartrain Park: abandoned property post-Katrina, **128**; accounts from residents riding out the storm: 20, 22–26; African American entertainers from, 32; as an African American middle-class neighborhood, xii, 5, 9, 32, 41–44, 133; and the American Dream, 41–44; attending New Orleans City Council meetings, 102–103; demographic changes in, 2000–2010, 125–127, **126**; demographics of, 32, 41–42; on differences in material circumstances, 33–34; and "elevation grant game," 102–104; and evacuation narratives, 63, 70; and exile narratives, 67–68, 70–71, 72; family and connection to place, 65–66; FEMA and disaster assistance narratives, 85, 86, 87, 89; first-person narratives on Katrina evacuation, 54–55, 56, 57; geography of, 41–43; history of, xii, 32, 36, 41–44, 69; housing styles of, 41; inspecting flood-damaged homes narratives, 100; and the "Katrina effect," 118, 119; and the legacy of Hurricane Katrina, 117; living in exile and the scarlet letter "E," 66–68; maps of, **35**, **43**; narratives on FEMA's response, 81–82; navigating the "Kafkaesque" bureaucracy of the Road Home Program, 96–97; and overview of first-person narratives, 46–48; personal reflections on race, 12; quality of neighborhood life post-Katrina, 125–127; race and class, 41–44; rebuilding narratives, 104, 111;

rebuilt house post-Katrina, **112**; recovery and the "editing" of life post-Katrina, 129–132; separate but equal, xii, 41–42

post-traumatic stress disorder (PTSD): and the "Katrina effect," 120–123

poverty line: in New Orleans, xi–xii

Powell, Lawrence: on New Orleans' rebuilding failure post-Katrina, 101–102

public assistance (PA) funding, 84. *See also* disaster assistance; Public Law 91-79 (1969)

Public Law 91-79 (1969), 83–84

race: and African American homeowners' class-action lawsuit against Road Home Program, 97–98; language of, and looting, 142n8; and New Orleans' neighborhoods, 31; personal reflections on, 11–12; question of, and government response to Hurricane Katrina, 45–46

Rand, Ayn: on collectivism, 90, 91

rebuilding of New Orleans, 75, 107–114; and Bring New Orleans Back initiative, 105–106; and City of New Orleans' lack of urban recovery plans, 101–102, 108; and class-action lawsuit against Road Home Program, 97–98; and damage assessments, 104–105; and disaster relief creating a "second disaster," 115, 151n20; and "elevation grant game," 102–104; and federal assistance, 84; and FEMA's allocation of rebuilding funds, 104–105; and homeowners' "go-it-alone" attitude, 105, 106–107; and homeowners versus contractors, 107–114; and mayor's misallocation of federal dollars for, 102; and recovery process at one-year anniversary of Katrina, 101–102; and suspension of Davis-Bacon Act, 90–91. *See also* disaster assistance; Hollygrove; homeowners; Kafkaesque; Pontchartrain Park

recovery. *See* disaster recovery; rebuilding

recovery assistance. *See* disaster assistance; insurance companies

Red Cross, 84, 85, 88

red tape. *See* Kafkaesque

renters: exclusion from Road Home Program, 93; and federal disaster assistance, 79–80, 93; seeking disaster assistance and parallel to Alice's adventures in Wonderland, 81, 98

resilience, of community in disaster recovery, 136–137, 153n10. *See also* disaster recovery; go-it-alone attitude; rebuilding

Road Home Program, 120, 133; and class-action lawsuit against, 97–98; description of, 91–92; and elevation requirements, 103–104; and Hazard Mitigation Grant funds, 104, 106; homeowners' narratives on applying for assistance from, 87, 89, 102–103; navigating the "Kafkaesque" bureaucracy of the Road Home Program, 93–97; and parallel to Alice's adventures in Wonderland, 81, 95, 98. *See also* disaster assistance; insurance companies; Kafkaesque

Roemer, Michael: on the literary hero, 48

Roosevelt, Franklin Delano: and social democracy, 90

river: being "sold down the —," xi

San Francisco 1906 earthquake and fire, 82–83, 140n11; compared to Hurricane Katrina disaster, 105, 151n20

Sartre, Jean-Paul: on metastable and the exiled world, 75, 146n18

scarlet letter "E": and life in exile, 66–68

Schopenhauer, Arthur, 95

Schutz, Alfred: on the effects of the unforeseen, 19

segregation: and Pontchartrain Park, 41–43

separate but equal: and Pontchartrain Park, xii, 41–42

Shaw Group, 91, 107

Silvestri, Frank: and Citizens Road Home Action Group, 92

slavery: and antebellum New Orleans, xi; and being "sold down the river," xi

social order: and the unpredictability of human life, 134–135

space: contingency of, 75

Stack, Carol: and her study on poor urban black families, 141n20

"strangeness, first-day," and the Mississippi River flood of 1927, 18–19

Strock, General Carl, 17

subcontractors. *See* contractors and subcontractors; rebuilding

Sununu, John, 91

Terkel, Studs: on the significance of conversation on human suffering, 141n13

Times-Picayune (New Orleans newspaper), 20, 101; front page headline for August 28, 2005, **18**

"To Whom It May Concern," addressing the audience question with, 7, 141n19

Twelve Years a Slave (Northup), xi

Uncle Tom's Cabin (Stowe), xi

unemployment payments. *See* disaster unemployment payments, 84

Urban Land Institute, 105

Vieux Carré: Bienville and the, 3. *See also* French Quarter

"When the Levee Breaks" (song), 51

white flight, to the suburbs, 40

Wilson, William Julius: on race and opportunity, 144n4

working-class neighborhood. *See* Hollygrove

World Meteorological Organization (WMO): and the retirement of "Katrina" as a hurricane name, 132

Wright, Richard, and "first-day strangeness," 18–19

zone of insecurity: and William James, 2